M000002984

Close Encounters
with
Deadly Dangers

Close Encounters with Deadly Dangers

Riveting Reads and Classroom Ideas

Kendall Haven

1999
Libraries Unlimited, Inc.
and its division
Teacher Ideas Press
Englewood, Colorado

Copyright © 1999 Kendall Haven
All Rights Reserved
Printed in the United States of America

No part of this publication may be reproduced, stored in a retrieval system, or transmitted, in any form or by any means, electronic, mechanical, photocopying, recording, or otherwise, without the prior written permission of the publisher.

LIBRARIES UNLIMITED, INC.
and its division
Teacher Ideas Press
P.O. Box 6633
Englewood, CO 80155-6633
1-800-237-6124
www.lu.com

Production Editor: Kevin W. Perizzolo
Copy Editor: Sharon DeJohn
Proofreader: Susie Sigman
Indexer: Linda Running Bentley
Typesetter: Kay Minnis

Library of Congress Cataloging-in-Publication Data

Haven, Kendall F.
  Close encounters with deadly dangers : riveting reads and classroom ideas / Kendall Haven.
    xv, 149 p. 17x25 cm.
  Includes bibliographical references and index.
  ISBN 1-56308-653-0 (softbound)
  1. Predatory animals. 2. Biotic communities. 3. Predatory animals--Study and teaching. 4. Biotic communities--Study and teaching. I. Title.
QL758.H38   1998
591.5'3--dc21   98-41353
                                                              CIP

To the countless thousands of field and lab workers
who have dedicated years and lifetimes
to the diligent and painstaking study
of each and every species, niche, relationship, and ecosystem on earth.
The information they have wrested from our natural surroundings
comes with a very heavy price tag of human effort, toil, and energy,
which they freely gave to give us
the priceless gifts of knowledge and understanding.

Contents

Squeeze Play

A "Croc" of Jaws

Treacherous Tusks

Stories from
Terrestrial Ecosystems

Death by Numbers

Introduction

I was once asked to tell stories at a fourth-grade nature camp. I accepted, expecting to tell chilling ghost stories around a flickering campfire. I later learned they expected me to tell natural environmental stories. I wasn't even sure where "natural environmental stories" stopped, and other stories, such as natural ghost stories began.

Under the watchful eye of the curmudgeonly camp director, I decided to abandon "The Monkey's Paw" and play it safe by telling about an African plain ecosystem such as the famed Serengeti plain. I started by describing endless miles of waving, yellow savanna grass under a relentless tropical sun. Sixty fourth graders fidgeted as they sat cross-legged on the floor.

My story dropped below the waving grass of the plain, describing two enterprising dung beetles busily returning waste to new soil. I followed a cautious field mouse nibbling her way through fallen grass seeds, pausing every few bites to listen and smell for signs of danger.

I got the first muttered complaints from the crowd. "Yeah, yeah. Get on with it. What *happens*?" Several girls looked confused, as if this wasn't what they had envisioned when their camp counselor said to gather for stories.

I described a curving line of black ants swarming over the crumpled remains of a dead bird.

"Forget the ants," demanded one boy. "How big was the bird? Who killed it? A cheetah? A lion?" Instantly all eyes lit with a smoldering fire of anticipation.

No, I told them. It just died and the ants ate it. I described the tentative hooves of an impala tip-toeing through the grass as if trying to be invisible.

"But what *happens*?" repeated the boy in the front row. Two of his friends nodded threateningly next to him.

I told how the impala nibbled and trotted on. It was normal, busy life happening, just like every day.

"That's *it*?" complained several more children. "No one gets *killed*?!"

I caved in and said that, at that moment, the heavy paw of a snarling lion trampled the grass.

I saw the teeth clench, the eyes glow to life, the fists clench, "Yeah! Here comes the story!"

The lion's hot breath blew across the plain like waves of gnawing fear. The great hunter was on the prowl. He planned to kill.

The front-row boy high-fived one of his friends. "All right! Finally! We get to the good part!"

It seems we are all fascinated by top predators and by the deadly drama of the hunt. Maybe it's because we are a top predator, ourselves. Maybe it's because big predators look, feel, and act dangerous, deadly dangerous. Maybe it is because vicariously we thrill to the call of the hunt.

Top predators are no better, no more interesting, no more important than any other part of the whole ecosystem. The lion and the bark beetle each have a unique and equally important part to play. They are both cooperating parts of the same system. They depend on each other, just as every individual, species, and community within an ecosystem depends on every other to fulfill its role in supporting the entire system.

What is an ecosystem? It is an interacting system made up of biological communities and non-living surroundings within a fixed geographical area. An ecosystem is the flora, the fauna, the land, the water, the topography, the environment, and the climate.

An individual ladybug is part of a population of ladybugs, which prey on certain other insects and are preyed upon by other insects and birds. This interacting group of species forms a community within a limited, physical portion of the whole environment, in this case, the bramble or bush community. That community combines with many other communities and with the flow of water, heat, light, and chemical nutrients to create a woodland ecosystem.

An ecosystem is an interdependent system. No species exists alone. Ecosystems require every niche to be actively, successfully occupied if the system is to survive. They need nutrients and dirt, plants, grazers, predators, scavengers, and finally decomposers to turn it all back into dirt and nutrients again. From outside the system, sunlight, heat, and water must continually flow into and through the ecosystem.

Every species depends on others, as prey, as predator, and to maintain the complete cyclical flow of matter and life through the system. Prey depend on predators almost as much as predators depend on prey if stable populations are to be preserved.

So why create a collection of stories about major predators in different environments and ecosystems? Because they're more fun! We love BIG, DANGEROUS predators. We love them but we also hate them and fear them. Maybe we are in awe of their power and ferocity, their toughness, their ability to survive. Maybe we recognize a piece of ourselves in their snarling attempts to master their environment.

Really, of course, most insects and animals are predators. Ladybugs eat aphids and are predators. Robins eat worms and are predators. Colorful tropical fish eat smaller fish and zooplankton. They are all predators. But they aren't dangerous to humans. And it is stories of dangerous predators that thrill us to the core.

This collection of stories, then, has two purposes. First, to provide scientifically accurate, detailed information about 17 of the world's deadliest predators in exciting story form. (The first story discusses two predators.) Second, to use these stories to introduce an exploration of the ecosystems that support these predators and of the countless host of less glamorous, but equally important, members of these ecosystems. Stories about any member of an ecosystem are really stories about the dynamics of the entire ecosystem, and they bring to light a host of questions about how that system works.

Let the stories begin their work as fascinating, spine-tingling journeys on the hunt with each predator. But the stories fulfill their real purpose only when they lead the reader to further explore interdependencies within an ecosystem and ecosystem dynamics as a whole.

It was difficult to select 16 deadly dangers from the hundreds of possible candidates. I tried to represent a wide variety of ecosystems and types of predators. Six of the stories are of aquatic habitats (two from saltwater, four from freshwater systems). Ten are from terrestrial systems. These range across most of the major continents and include insects, snakes, giant lizards, birds of prey, reptiles, and well-known mammal predators. They include desert, meadow, woodland, mountain, Arctic tundra, savanna, pine forest, and rain forest environments.

In researching and writing these stories I became acutely aware of a massive debt I in particular, and all of us in general, owe to those who have studied natural environments and their wildlife. An incredible amount of dedicated effort is required to wrestle each secret from nature. To learn about just one species is a monumental task. Teams of researchers have spent lifetimes tracking, cataloging, studying, and documenting the behavior, food preferences, territorial and ecosystem needs, and lifecycle information for two specific wolf packs on one small island in Northeast Canada. Hundreds of other teams have dedicated equal amounts of time and thoughtful attention to other wolf families scattered across the continent. Many of these field studies lasted for 30 years or more.

Groups of other biological researchers have meticulously studied wolf physiology and chemistry to determine the physical abilities and properties of this species. Specialized researchers have analyzed their communication systems and their vocal calls.

The mountains of resulting data had to be synthesized, assessed, and translated into useful information by scores of other researchers. Thousands of human careers over a century of study have been dedicated to studying the wolf in order to give us even the most basic understanding of this glorious creature.

There are tens of thousands of species and hundreds of ecosystems, each with its own unique relationships and peculiarities. My stories represent the successful end product of the dedicated research of literally hundreds of thousands of field researchers, lab researchers and technicians, and data analysts. We all owe these unheralded scientists great thanks. They have translated the sweat of their brows into understanding and have freely given it to us.

Finally, Roni Berg has once again acted as the true litmus test for these stories. With uncanny accuracy and profound insight she has helped to focus each story and ensure that each stayed true to its ultimate purpose and reached its most exciting and fascinating potential. I owe her an unending debt of gratitude.

Enjoy the stories. Enjoy exploring the ecosystem and predator questions following each story. But above all else, let these stories kindle your own fascination for the never-ending wonders of nature. Explore, ponder, poke, and prod in your own local environment. Finally, create your own stories and design your own explorations. The joy and intrigue never ends!

How to Use This Book

The stories in this book are divided into two sections: stories from aquatic ecosystems (both fresh- and saltwater systems), and from terrestrial systems, including desert, meadow, woodland, mountain, Arctic tundra, savanna, pine forest, and jungle ecosystems.

I am often asked if my stories are true. Did they really happen?

All predator and prey behavior, traits, biology, and relationships presented in these stories are typical of the documented traits of the species involved and are based on extensive documented field and laboratory studies. They are true in that every event and activity presented in these stories happens regularly as a natural part of the ecosystem. That is, I created these characters to be representative of the normal behavior of their species and typical of their environment. There is no event here that hasn't happened countless thousands of times. But I have not personally witnessed any of these events. I had to envision (imagine) the specific encounters, characters, and interactions reported in these stories for myself based on available research. Thus, the specifics of each story are fictional. Still, all of the information in each story may be relied upon as representing the best understanding we have of that species and its interaction with its environment and ecosystem.

Three brief sections follow each story: "Thinking About This Ecosystem," "Thinking About This Predator," and "Additional Reading." The questions, answers, and suggested activities and research in these sections are designed to help teachers and students explore the concepts and information presented in the story. Specifically, questions will lead to understanding ecosystem relationships and development, survival strategies of various plant and animal components of an ecosystem, interdependencies and cooperative relationships within an ecosystem, and the interdependencies of predator and prey species.

Additionally, I have used these sections to include significant and interesting predator information that was not included in the body of the story.

Finally, I have included children's and adult listings in the bibliography for both species-specific references for the main predator of the story and the ecosystem as a whole.

Stories from Aquatic Ecosystems

A Whale of a Fight

Sperm Whales and Giant Squids of the Pacific Ocean

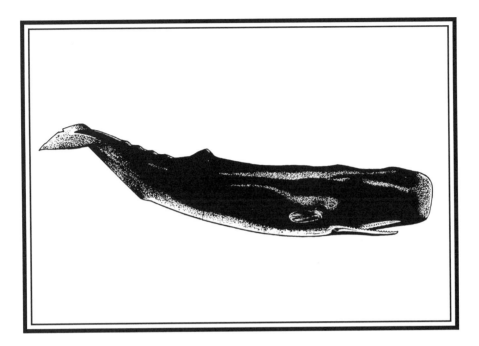

At a Glance

When we think of whales we think BIG. We think of humped backs rolling to the surface to breathe, spouting steamy clouds of vapor into the air. Most whales are filter feeders. They don't eat fish, but rather filter tiny plankton, called krill, from the water. During the peak feeding season, a whale will eat tons of krill a day. The Pacific humpback whale and the giant blue whale are examples of filter-feeding whales. (The latter is the largest living creature in the history of the Earth.)

A few whale species are true carnivores and predators. They eat fish, squid, and seals. Killer whales, narwhals, and sperm whales all have jaws and teeth and eat fish. The sperm whale is by far the biggest and best known of the carnivorous whales. Moby Dick was a sperm whale.

Great sperm whales, swimming free through the deep blue oceans, have only two enemies: man and giant squids.

3

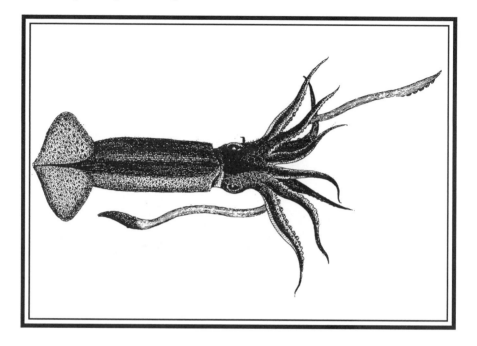

The giant squid is a true mystery creature of the deep. Its long, twisting tentacles probably account for most sightings of "sea serpents." Giant squid live solitary lives in deep, lightless oceans. They are rarely seen at the surface. They are very rarely seen by man. Individual giant squid have been caught that measure well over 100 feet in length. Evidence exists of giants over twice that length.

Sperm whales and giant squid, like the Hatfields and the McCoys, are natural enemies. They compete for the same food and the same territory. More than that, there seems to be a natural grudge between these two species that makes them want to fight. Watching a brawl between these two behemoths of the oceans would have to be one of the most spectacular sights in the natural world. Such a battle would truly deserve the title: "the biggest show on earth!"

"A Whale of a Fight"

The sperm whale calf dips into a shallow dive, blue-green light dancing in curtain-like waves around him. He glides with no conscious effort through the endless expanse of clear Pacific Ocean water 800 miles west of Mexico. It is early October. He is exactly one month old. From a birth weight of one ton, his weight has doubled to over two tons and his length has stretched to over 18 feet.

Next to him his mother glides at peace under a tropical sun that dips steadily toward the western horizon. At 40 feet and 22 tons, she is longer than a school bus and weighs as much as 20 elephants, about average for the hundreds of females in the great whale herd feeding, loafing, playing, and even quarreling through a 1,000-mile circle near the equator. Water streams off her dark gray skin as her back arches above the water line. With a whoosh! she blows a vapor cloud into the cloudless sky as she exhales, her back glistening in the sunlight before it dips back beneath the rocking waves.

The calf's skin will be almost pure black, but is still covered with the light pink wash of youth. His exhalations do not yet rumble through the water like distant thunder (as do those of the head male, or "bull" of this family, a 50-ton monster), even though he tries with all his might and wishes they would.

The mother breathes deeply several times, raises her tail high in the air to gain momentum, and curves into a vertical plunge into the ink-black depths. The calf is left, anxious, at the surface. Although she dives three or four times a day for food, he still feels uneasy being abandoned for up to an hour while she feeds.

Sperm whales are timid and run at any sign of trouble. But they are also hunters, living on the fish and squid they catch. The gaping lower jaw of an adult swings open like a gate, taller than two full-grown people, exposing 60 teeth, each as big as a human head. These teeth aren't razor sharp like a shark's, but are backed by enough muscle to crush and grind through any resistance.

The calf dives behind his mother, not to follow—he is still too fragile and weak for deep dives—but to be comforted by the countless high-frequency ultrasounds of a thousand whales communicating with each other across the miles, holding the herd together with

From *Close Encounters with Deadly Dangers*. © 1998 Kendall Haven. Libraries Unlimited. (800) 237-6124.

invisible ultrasound strings. Far from being an empty desert, the open ocean is filled with life and a symphony of sounds. Few of these sights and sounds, however, rise to the water's surface, so that the quiet, empty air above the ocean makes it appear to be deserted.

As the calf surfaces to breathe, a two-year-old male soars into the air from below, his blunt, square-nosed body silhouetted against the reds and oranges of sunset as he hangs for a moment, almost balanced on his broad tail. With a half twist, the whale crashes to the sea with a noise like thunder, shooting waves of spray across the ocean.

Two friends follow suit. The calf realizes it is a game, a game he will soon be strong enough to play.

One-quarter mile below the calf another hunter cruises through a world of permanent black in search of prey. Life here is lived by sound, smell, and feel. Eyes are useless in the lightless depths, though this killer has the largest eyes in the world in its soft, balloon-shaped head, each eyeball larger than a basketball. This predator is at home in the black, a jet-powered hunter with more speed, maneuverability, and raw grabbing power than any other creature in the ocean. No shark would stand a chance against this killer. It is also timid, even shy, even though it is one of the world's most vicious hunters and fighters. By name, this predator is called a giant squid.

This squid weighs over four tons and measures 120 feet, the length of four school buses, from the tip of its arrow-shaped tail to its two elongated arms that ripple like sea serpents far in front of the squid's body. This squid is longer than the biggest dinosaur that ever walked the earth, but is only average sized for its elusive species.

Teeth-ringed suckers on its two long arms allow the squid to lock onto any prey. Eight shorter tentacles, each as thick as a grown person's body, dangle in a circle around the two long arms, looking like ten-foot, wiggling snakes. The tentacles seem to paw the water as if waiting for a chance to wrap around some tender treat and pull it into the rock-hard, razor-sharp beak, as big across as a grown human's arm is long. Nothing else in the ocean can grab, twist, squeeze, crush, and hold as can the giant squid.

Squids don't swim. They soar through the water. A squid sucks water into its body cavity and then blasts it back out through two narrow side funnels (called *siphons*) at high speed. This exhaust water rockets a squid in the same way that exhaust gases power a jet. Unlike

From *Close Encounters with Deadly Dangers*. © 1998 Kendall Haven. Libraries Unlimited. (800) 237-6124.

a jet, though, the squid moves backwards, arrow tail first, torpedo-shaped body next, 80-foot arms trailing behind.

Huge, luminescent black eyes stare into the black, but deep below the surface the squid hunts by vibration and sound, not by sight. The squid is hungry and decides to search up higher tonight, up where its eyes can help guide the final attack. Giant squids live their solitary lives in the ocean depths, eating fish, eels, swordfish, sharks, and even whales, and rise to feed in the near-surface waters only when rich plankton fields draw other sea creatures closer to the surface.

At the surface the calf's mother bursts through the water with a hissing vapor cloud of exhalation. Two albacore tuna are still caught between her mighty jaws. With clicks, squeaks, and song-like whines the calf races to his mother's side, relieved and comforted by her presence. He does not eat solid food yet, and will live for months yet on his mother's milk.

A full moon has risen, throwing its reflection bright and sharp across the calm water as if molten silver had been poured across the waves.

The mother whale circles slowly around while she breathes deeply in and out, 50 times or more to recover from her dive. The calf knows she is about to dive again. Her sonar must have found a large school of fish in the mysterious depths, which the calf has never seen.

With a flick of her tail the mother dips into a second deep dive. The calf follows, frantically beating its broad tail to keep up with her as she sounds. He knows he can't yet tolerate the pressure of the depths and has not yet developed the stamina for long dives, but the stirring deep within him makes him try.

Soon, he thinks to himself. *Soon it will be my turn.*

But for now he turns back to the nighttime surface of the sea, waiting again for his mother.

As she dives past 1,000 feet, past 1,500 feet, the mother whale sprays out sonar clicks into the lightless waters. She turns hard left and angles more shallowly, sensing the returning echo from one of her pings that has bounced off a moving object. Dolphins use a similar sonar system for detecting nearby objects, as do submarines.

The pattern of returning pings describes a large, soft, moving mass, perhaps a tight-packed school of fish. To the mother whale, the pings describe dinner.

From *Close Encounters with Deadly Dangers*. © 1998 Kendall Haven. Libraries Unlimited. (800) 237-6124.

The giant squid senses the impending collision, the impact, before the mother whale. With high-pressure jet siphons it spins in a tight circle, its arrow-shaped tail to the rear, deadly arms and beak to the attack.

Before the sperm whale can open her jaw and roll slightly into feeding position, the immense bodies collide, she speeding downward at 18 miles an hour, the squid racing up at 20. The water shakes from the force of their meeting. The squid's long arms wrap tightly around the whale's head. The suction cups on its shorter tentacles, like pieces of cellophane tape, lock the whale's mighty jaw shut.

As the bodies collide, the squid's beak is driven forward, snapping shut to tear away a small piece of whale skin and the white blubber below.

The mother's heart pounds. Adrenaline surges through her body. She thrashes wildly, trying to shake the squid's deadly grip, trying to crush it with a blow from her mighty tail.

But the squid is wise. It knows how to win this fight of giants: keep its body away from the whale's tail, keep her jaw locked shut, and hold her underwater until she weakens and drowns. Again its beak pecks forward, tearing a second piece of flesh from above her left eye.

The squid propels downward with its high-powered jets toward the black depths, squeezing the whale with all its might. The razor teeth of its suction cups cut into her skin, leaving deep circles branded into her flesh.

Soon the whale will need to breathe. If it can keep her from the surface, she will tire and weaken. A battle that started as two competitors fighting over feeding rights has become a deadly duel. One will survive victorious, one will die.

Desperately the mother whale spins and twists, forcing the squid to strain just to hold on. With all her might she powers toward the waiting starlight above. The squid, still locked tight to her head, uses its jet siphons to slow her assent, tire her out, and drag her down.

One thousand feet to the surface. Eight hundred feet. The whale's lungs burn. Her heart pounds so hard it rattles her mammoth rib cage. Five hundred feet. Four hundred feet. She feels a desperate, overwhelming need to breathe. Three hundred feet. Two hundred feet. Her vision blurs as her oxygen supply runs out.

From *Close Encounters with Deadly Dangers*. © 1998 Kendall Haven. Libraries Unlimited. (800) 237-6124.

The little calf jumps in fright as the water boils around him. Through the center of the seething foam his mother and the squid burst into the cool night air. The calf is caught between two strong desires: run *from* the turmoil, and run *to* his mother. He hesitates, tense and unsure, as the great bodies, almost as big as a house, crash and spin across the ocean.

Other sperm whales do not rush to the aid of their struggling sister. With sharp clicks of alarm they hover well out of harm's way, tensely awaiting the outcome.

Again the combatants explode through the water's surface as if to throw themselves into the sky. The squid still locks its arms tight around the whale, holding on like a rodeo rider, still hoping to exhaust and overpower its victim. Again they crash to the surface in a thunderclap of spray.

With a wrenching twist, the mother throws the squid's body back along her side. At last her chance has come. With a stinging slap that could crush the side of a wooden sailing ship, she bangs the squid with her massive tail.

The squid's grip is loosened by the blow. The whale's jaw twists free, swinging open like the mighty gates of doom.

Now it is her turn to fly into the attack. In a thrashing twist, her jaws clamp down on one of the squid's long arms and on two of its shorter tentacles. Locked in a crushing vice, the attacker has become the victim.

A frenzied thicket of living limbs claws around the whale's lips, twisting and snapping like a dozen writhing snakes, like the elongated fingers of some giant's hands.

The squid again turns its siphons to jet-powered propulsion in a desperate attempt to flee a losing battle.

The whale's teeth grind down. She shakes her prey as if it were a flopping rag doll, as if to communicate her fury.

The squid breaks loose during a violent shake of her head. It squirts gallons of jet-black ink to mask its escape trail and flees in tormented retreat toward the safety of the depths. It is badly wounded and weak. But it has survived for now.

The mother whale's tail thrashes the water with both relief and frustration. She has escaped a deadly ambush, but her meal has also

From *Close Encounters with Deadly Dangers.* © 1998 Kendall Haven. Libraries Unlimited. (800) 237-6124.

escaped. She is too tired to pursue the injured squid and dares not dive again until her breathing slows and her heart calms.

The sea around her returns to calm as her calf rushes to her side. His life still depends on her; her danger was his danger. She has been lucky: The bites and pockmarks from suckers are shallow and will heal.

The calf smells the oils and nectar of the squid in the wake of the battle. He can taste bits of squid flesh lingering on the surface. Boldly he dives after the squid, as if to yell, "And stay out!"

Diving deeper and deeper to levels new and strange to him, he can feel the weight of water above press on his muscles, squeeze his organs, and make his tendons groan. The tingling exhilaration tells him he will someday be master of all this world.

The calf roars back to the surface, breaching in a great, foaming wave. He snorts a vapor cloud.

The sound rumbles through the depths like distant thunder.

Thinking About This Ecosystem

Is the open ocean a separate ecosystem? What are its bounds? How is this ecosystem different from the coastal, or shallow water, ocean ecosystem? (*Compare depth of water, temperature of water, nutrient supply, and species diversity and density.*) Do different fish live in coastal and open-ocean ecosystems? What plants and animals live in the coastal zone that don't live in the open ocean? (*Remember to include inter-tidal species, such as clams, mussels, and starfish, and coastal crustaceans, such as crabs, lobsters, and shrimp.*)

All ecosystems depend on a stable supply of plants. What plants grow in the ocean? (*Kelp, algae, and plankton.*) Have you heard the term *plankton*? There are two kinds of plankton, phytoplankton and zooplankton. See if you can find the difference between them. Which are true plants? Which are tiny animals?

Plants depend on light, water, heat, and nutrients. What nutrients do plants need most? (*What are the three major components of any fertilizer?*) Are these more available near the coasts or in the deep oceans? (*Definitely near the coasts, where upwelling of nutrient-rich bottom water brings nutrients to the surface where heat and sunlight exist.*)

How is the open-ocean ecosystem similar to a desert? (*Deserts have few plants.*) What limits plant growth in a terrestrial desert? In an ocean desert? (*Most often a lack of water limits land-based desert growth while a lack of nutrients limits ocean plant growth.*)

From *Close Encounters with Deadly Dangers.* © 1998 Kendall Haven. Libraries Unlimited. (800) 237-6124.

Like a terrestrial desert, the open ocean does support many animals, in this case fish and mammals. Make a list of the major open-ocean fish and mammal species. How many live near the surface? How many live in the deep ocean where light and plant life do not exist? What do they eat?

Thinking About This Predator

Giant squid are most interesting predators, because we know so little about them and because what little we do know about them is fascinating. We don't know how many there are. We don't really know how big they can grow. We know very little about their life cycle (where they mate, where they give birth, how long they live, etc.). The best basic life-cycle information for the giant squid comes from studying small, coastal squid. The big question about the usability of this information is, How similar are a one-pound coastal squid and a 10- to 20-ton deep ocean giant squid?

In this battle the squid lost and most likely died a quiet, unseen death in the chilly depths. The sperm whale triumphed. These two giants of the open ocean are natural, mortal enemies. They compete for the same food. They attack and kill each other.

Oceanographers believe that the sperm whale wins the fight far more often than it loses. When the squid wins and the whale dies, there is no evidence to tell the tale. We have no record of the event, so we will never know for sure.

When the whale wins and survives, circular pockmarks from the squid's suckers are left, forever scarred into the whale's flesh. The squid in this story measured 120 feet, tip to tip, and left pockmarks on the whale's head four to six inches across.

Sperm whales have been caught with pockmarks from bigger squid measuring over *18* inches across. The squid that made those marks would measure over 200 feet, or over seven school buses, in length, and would weigh around 30 tons!

Unfortunately, both these species are now rare in our world, having been hunted to near extinction. They are two wondrous members of the top of the open-ocean ecosystem that few humans will ever have the privilege to see.

See if you can find additional information about these two great beasts of the ocean at your library, on the Internet, or through oceanography departments of local universities. Here are some questions you can use to start your research:

1. Why do you think giant squid live virtually all of their lives in the lightless depths of the ocean? What do they gain from living where no other big predators live?

2. What do sperm whales and giant squid gain from being big? Bigger organisms need more food each day. What are the advantages and disadvantages of being big?

Additional Reading

Here are references for information about sperm whales, giant squid, and the open-ocean ecosystem. See your librarian for additional titles available at your local library.

Angel, Heather. *Life in the Oceans: The Spectacular World of Whales, Giant Squid, Sharks and Other Unusual Sea Creatures.* New York: Bookthrift, 1976.

Bunting, Eve. *The Giant Squid.* New York: Julian Messner, 1981.

Burton, Robert. *The Life and Death of Whales.* London: Andre Deutsch, 1980.

Cousteau, Jacques. *Octopus and Squid, the Soft Intelligence.* Garden City, NY: Doubleday, 1973.

Ellis, Richard. *The Book of Whales.* New York: Alfred A. Knopf, 1980.

———. *Men and Whales.* New York: Alfred A. Knopf, 1991.

Garcia, Eulalia. *Giant Squid: Monsters of the Deep.* Milwaukee, WI: Gareth Stevens, 1997.

McClung, Robert. *Thor, Last of the Sperm Whales.* New York: William Morrow, 1971.

Minasian, Stanley. *The World's Whales.* Washington, DC: Smithsonian Books, 1984.

Mowat, Farley. *A Whale for the Killing.* Boston: Little, Brown, 1972.

Scheffer, Victor. *The Year of the Whale.* New York: Charles Scribner's Sons, 1969.

———. *Little Calf.* New York: Charles Scribner's Sons, 1970.

Slijpin, Everhard. *Whales.* Ithaca, NY: Cornell University Press, 1979.

Utah State University Department of Wildlife. *Sperm Whale Population Analysis.* Washington, DC: Marine Mammal Commission, 1982.

Whitehead, Hal. *Voyage to the Whales.* Post Mills, VT: Chelsea Green Publication, 1990.

Tiger Jaws

Tiger Sharks of Pacific Tropical Reefs

At a Glance

Many people shudder when they think of sharks. Images from movies like *Jaws* flash through their minds, images of a senseless, brutal killer that rises silently from the invisible depths of the ocean to maim and destroy. Even the word *shark* supports this image. It comes from the German word *Schurke*, which means "villain."

Sharks are powerful. They have cold, pitiless, black eyes and rows of jagged, serrated teeth. Sharks seem savage, evil, and brutish.

In truth, while sharks are efficient and powerful top predators of the ocean environment, they are far from cruel. They are simply another member of a complex ecosystem trying to survive. To do that, they must eat. Sharks are carnivores, and so must feed on other fish and on mammals.

Sharks appear often in human folklore and mythology. They are God-like in the legends and stories from Hawaii and Polynesia. They appear often as pivotal characters in tales from ancient Greece and Babylon.

Over 300 species of sharks inhabit the world's oceans and seas. Only a dozen of these species are dangerous to man, and only three or four come to mind when we think of "shark." The most famous is the biggest of the man-eaters, the great white shark.

But a human is more likely to survive an encounter with a great white than with a tiger shark. Tiger sharks are smaller than the great white, but are more aggressive. They are also more territorial and prone to attack for the sake of the attack. A tiger shark patrolling a reef it has claimed as its own is one of the most dangerous creatures in the ocean.

"Tiger Jaws"

Gliding . . . forever effortlessly gliding through liquid blue. Swimming lazily, cruising without direction or pause, wandering across an endless world of three-dimensional, undulating curtains of shimmering blue light. Following minute chemical smells in the water, following whims, following the feel of warm water. Following faint sounds and vibrations, following the contours of the reef.

The shark swims mindlessly without stopping, day and night, on an endless, deadly hunt. The shark cannot float. The only fish without a swim bladder (an adjustable, gas-filled bladder that keeps fish in perfect balance with the water, neither floating up nor sinking un-less they want to), this creature would slowly sink if it stopped its end-less swim.

It must also forever move, or face into a moving current, in order to breathe. Again, unique among fish, this giant of the sea lacks the ability to suck in seawater and blow it out across its gills, the lungs of every fish. It must *move* through the water to make water flow across its gills, to breathe.

These are two of the three great differences between a shark and other fish. The third is that a shark has no bones. Its skeleton is made entirely of cartilage, like the bridge of a human nose. Cartilage, unlike bone, decays like skin after death. When a shark dies, all that is left is a pile of serrated, deadly teeth.

Swimming to float, swimming to breathe, day and night, every day, for all of its 30- to 40-year life span, the tiger shark lives a nomadic, solitary life. Named for the dark stripes along its back, an

From *Close Encounters with Deadly Dangers.* © 1998 Kendall Haven. Libraries Unlimited. (800) 237-6124.

adult tiger shark, ranging from 12 to 20 feet in length, is one of the world's deadliest predators.

Drifting day and night though twirling curtains of light, the tiger shark eats anytime, anywhere, and anything, ceaselessly hunting for whatever it can catch.

Fearlessly covering as much as 50 miles a day, with the coral reef below, the blazing white brilliance of the tropical sun above, and wavering blue curtains of water all around, this tiger shark has laid claim to a long reef one-quarter mile off the Mexican coast south of Acapulco. As it passes, all other species edge away, not wanting to flee and draw attention, watching warily as this shadow of doom passes by.

The time is January, winter in the northern hemisphere. In the summer, the tiger shark will drift north with the warm currents, wandering as far up the coast as Canada. But in the winter, tiger sharks hover over shallow tropical reefs. More territorial than most sharks, the tiger often lays claim to a reef for the whole winter, becoming a true nomad only in the summer.

By current estimates there are over a billion sharks in the world, divided among over 300 species. They range from the smallest dwarf shark, at six inches in length, to the whale shark, at over 50 feet. Sharks have swum the seas since before the earliest dinosaur set foot on land.

Only a dozen species of shark are truly dangerous to man. The great white shark is the most famous and accounts for more attacks on humans than any other. But the tiger shark is probably the fiercest. Tiger sharks are more aggressive and less hesitant to attack, less tentative in the initial biting than other sharks. They tend to eat all of a victim, biting over and over again until it is completely consumed. Most sharks, including great whites, tend to rip out one bite and move on to another victim.

Nothing in the sea is more dangerous than this tiger shark as it slowly cruises the reef, sensing minute chemical traces of distant food, "listening" for even the faintest, distant, erratic vibrations of a fish in trouble.

He is a male tiger shark, 18 feet long and weighing almost one and one-half tons. Besides humans, there are only two predators for this shark: giant squid and sperm whales. But neither of these creatures frequents shallow coastal reefs, so the shark hunts with supreme and fearless confidence.

From *Close Encounters with Deadly Dangers.* © 1998 Kendall Haven. Libraries Unlimited. (800) 237-6124.

His broad, blunt snout protrudes above a wide, curved mouth and his row of sharp, triangular, serrated teeth. His eyes are wide set and solid, lifeless black. His dark gray skin is more coarse than the roughest sandpaper and can tear the flesh off a human leg just by brushing past.

A faint trace smell, a few molecules of scent in a liter of water, makes the tiger turn left and nose higher along the reef. His tall tail beats harder, propelling him past craggy coral beauty. A shark's long-range sense of smell is as sensitive and accurate as that of any species on earth.

A small armada swims upward with the shark. Silver pilot fish dart close to his flanks. Remora fish have attached themselves like leeches to the shark's head and face. Both species follow the shark, hoping to live off the scraps from the tiger's feasting. The shark generally ignores them, allowing them to tag along. But both small fish know to remain ever-vigilant else they become part of the tiger's next meal.

Now the shark can feel the distant vibrations of rhythmically beating tails. It is a school of medium-sized fish. Like a second, long-distance set of ears, tiger sharks have long, liquid-filled tubes, called lateral lines, running the length of their bodies. These lines detect low-frequency vibrations from miles away. The regular beating of these fish tails attracts the shark, but do not stimulate a frenzied drive of hunger as would the erratic beat of a wounded fish or the smell of blood.

The shark moves purposefully, zigzagging back and forth to make sure he follows the strongest line of scent. At 50 yards the shark can see the school of jack fish with their silver sides and blue-black stripes on top. His long-range sensors are abandoned. Now the shark hones in on his prey using electrochemical receptors, small glands located near his mouth. Good only over short distances, these glands can detect even a faint muscular twitch of an intended victim and guide the shark flawlessly toward its meal.

Yet even now, the shark is instinctively cautious, almost timid. He circles wide around the school, spiraling ever closer. He searches for unfamiliar creatures or swimming patterns, probing for any hint of danger. If the vibration, smell, and look of this school of fish were unfamiliar to the shark, he might well dart forward and brush past the new prey to see how it reacts before daring to attack.

From *Close Encounters with Deadly Dangers.* © 1998 Kendall Haven. Libraries Unlimited. (800) 237-6124.

Sharks are brutal, vicious, and deadly, but they are not natural fighters. They do not want to endure struggle or combat to win a prized meal. They would rather wander off in search of an easier catch elsewhere.

The shark circles warily, hunting for signs of resistance.

Now he attacks. His powerful tail pounds through the water. The shark bolts forward like a speeding torpedo. Using sight and his electrochemical receptors, he targets two specific fish in the school.

As one, the fish turn, frantically fleeing the impending attack. But the shark is too swift. His jaws snap shut over two jack fish, severing the tail of one and the head of the other. The grinding crunch of the shark's jaws reverberates through the water.

The tiger shark's jaws close with the force of several tons of pressure per square inch, enough to easily snap through bone as casually as human teeth might snap a breadstick. His serrated teeth slice through flesh more easily than a fine steak knife slices through a well-done roast.

Violently, instinctively, the shark shakes its head from side to side. This both allows the shark to rip his first bite free from a bigger carcass and disorients his victim, preventing escape or retaliation.

Rolling his head upward, the shark swallows both fish whole.

Casually, leisurely, the shark turns to drift farther along the reef instead of pursuing the fleeing school. He has no need to exert the effort of a long chase or to clean up the leftover scraps. There will soon be more food for the picking.

Pilot fish rush in to fight over the floating scraps, then rush to rejoin their shark and be in position to feast on the leftovers from his next kill.

The tiger, like many sharks, attacks indiscriminately. Its favorite meals include squid, fish, sea turtles, and even smaller sharks. But license plates, five-gallon metal cans, boots, and even small blenders have been found in sharks' stomachs.

A tiger shark never fears breaking or losing one of its deadly teeth. Stacks of replacements lie behind each tooth, tucked against its gums like pages of a book awaiting their turn to flip into position in the jaw. Interestingly, each replacement tooth for a tiger shark is slightly larger than the one it replaces. Over the years, a shark's teeth grow bigger and more lethal.

From *Close Encounters with Deadly Dangers.* © 1998 Kendall Haven. Libraries Unlimited. (800) 237-6124.

Still hungry, the tiger senses, or feels, splashing vibrations half a mile ahead. His stomach juices begin to churn. The smell of porpoise wafts strong through the water. The combination of smell and vibrations produce an unstoppable urge, a calling, an instinctive demand for the shark to eat, to kill, to attack.

Swimming hard, the tiger shark rises to the late afternoon surface of the Pacific. His slightly curved dorsal fin slices through the calm waters, casting up a small wave as would the bow of a boat.

Ahead he senses the presence of a small family of porpoise, flopping, splashing, and playing in the water. The tiger circles wide, searching for a pup, which is easier to attack than a full-grown adult.

He senses two of them.

Silently he glides below the surface. The best attacks come as total surprises from below. The tiger shark drifts cautiously closer. A group of adult porpoises can gang up on a shark, battering it with their hard noses, and crushing the shark's internal organs.

The tiger glides closer, circling along the reef, measuring the speed and position of each porpoise with his mid-range electrochemical receptors. His lateral lines detect the awkward splashing of a young porpoise trying to leap clear of the water, as the adults do so often in their play.

The pup is momentarily unguarded by adults as they romp, unaware of the danger swiftly closing in from below.

Again the pup tries to breach, lifting its tail as it soars into the air.

Thrashing his mighty tail, the tiger shark drives forward, rushing to meet the pup where it will crash back into the water.

The adults become aware of the charging shark. With squeals and clicks of alarm they rush to the pup's defense. Though only five feet long, and less than a quarter the shark's size, porpoises are faster, more maneuverable, and fiercely protective.

The pup giddily crashes back into the water, thrilled at its first successful breach. The tiger surges up from below on a beeline to the pup. The adults sprint to form a protective shield around the youth.

Falling down, down into the water column under its downward momentum, the pup hears the squeals of alarm and pipes out its own shrill cry.

From *Close Encounters with Deadly Dangers*. © 1998 Kendall Haven. Libraries Unlimited. (800) 237-6124.

With a final lunge the tiger catches the pup. Fearsome jaws lock onto the three-foot pup just ahead of its tail. Teeth grind and slice through tender porpoise hide, flesh, and bone.

The first of the adults, like a screeching rocket, slams into the shark's side at almost 50 miles per hour. The five-foot porpoise is dazed, and wallows drunkenly back through the water. The shark is knocked sideways, but maintains his grip on the youth.

With a violent twisting of his great head, the tiger shakes the pup like a dog shaking a bone. Blood flows thick into the water from the terrible gash deepening on the pup's side.

A second adult and now a third slam into the shark's body.

The shark does not feel the pain. He has no nervous system to detect and measure pain. Though the thundering blows from enraged porpoises have shattered rib cartilage and badly bruised several internal organs, the shark has smelled blood and is in a frenzy to feed.

Again the tiger violently shakes the pup in an attempt to kill or stun it. He releases his hold to swallow the first small bite he has ripped from the pup's flank.

Simultaneously five adult porpoises crash into the shark's tough hide like racing motorcycles slamming into a stalled pickup truck. The porpoises' noses are scraped and bloodied by the shark's rough skin.

Stunned, the shark is rolled backwards by the blow. His tail responds sluggishly because the porpoises have damaged part of his spinal column.

The pup is forgotten. The tiger flounders back into the deep along the front wall of the reef. The porpoises huddle around the wounded pup, nursing, reassuring it.

The pup is badly hurt, but it will survive.

The tiger shark, a magnificent killing machine perfected over countless millennia of evolution, will require weeks to recover from its injuries. But already his thoughts have returned to the next hunt and the next meal.

———

From *Close Encounters with Deadly Dangers*. © 1998 Kendall Haven. Libraries Unlimited. (800) 237-6124.

Thinking About This Ecosystem

Coral reefs are a unique environment. What is coral? (*Coral are animals, not plants, which live in large colonies. The rock-like formations we see and call coral are the secreted shells of generation upon generation of coral, all piled on top of each other.*) What makes coral reefs such rich and densely populated habitats? (*These reefs are shallow, warm, nutrient-rich environments where fixed plants such as fans, sponges, plankton, and other coastal plants can proliferate. Where plants are plentiful, grazers [fish who eat plants] will also be plentiful. Where large schools of these small fish gather, bigger, carnivorous fish will also gather.*)

See how many of the major coastal reefs in the world you can locate. Mark them on a map. What commonalities can you find between these reefs and reef locations?

This story mentions two types of fish, pilot and remora, that swim, and live with tiger sharks. Their relationship with the shark is called *symbiotic*, which means that each species does something beneficial for the other so that each is better off for having the other around. Can you find out what a shark does for pilot fish and for remora? Can you figure out what pilot fish and remora do for the shark? Look for symbiotic relationships in other ecosystems. They abound in every ecosystem in the world.

Thinking About This Predator

Sharks are one of the oldest predators on earth. Shark species, remarkably similar to today's large predator sharks, existed while dinosaurs first roamed the earth. They have changed very little during the past 100 million years. Why do you think sharks have been so successful and have not had to evolve as most species have? (*While no one knows the exact reason, there are many factors which contribute to sharks' success. Some of the important factors include: there has been little change in the oceanic environment while terrestrial environments have changed radically. Sharks possess excellent hunting instincts and sensory systems, so they haven't needed to adapt. And, sharks have always had a plentiful food supply and so haven't needed to change the way they live to find food.*) How many more reasons can you find?

(*Other, less obvious factors may also contribute to sharks' success. Sharks are not deposited as eggs by the mother to develop on their own, as with most oceanic species. Sharks are born alive and are instantly capable of swimming, hunting, and eating, their first full set of teeth being ready and in position at birth. Long ago sharks learned to rely on the most accurate sensory system in the water, chemical smells, for long-range tracking. Two-thirds of a shark's brain is devoted to the sense of smell. Sharks hunt day and night, unlike almost every other major predator species on earth. Finally, a shark will eat anything, so that, as the food web around it changes, a shark's ability to hunt and eat is not affected.*)

Sharks have a reputation for random, capricious behavior. They skip one fish and attack the next. They attack and maul one bather, skip two next to that person, and then bite a third a short distance away. Do you think shark attacks are really random? (*Recent research shows that shark behavior is definitely not random. Shark attacks are driven by signals sent to the brain by complex electrochemical receptors that evaluate the sea around the shark. These receptors are often confused by metal and other man-made objects, so the shark's resulting behavior appears to be erratic. There are a few well-known triggers that draw sharks and encourage attack: blood in the water, erratic splashing, feeble splashing or vibrations, and floundering.*)

Are sharks a major danger when going to the beach? See if you can find statistics at your library to determine how many Americans die or are injured each year from each of the following dangers associated with a trip to the ocean: shark attacks; drowning in the ocean; boating accidents; scuba diving accidents; getting seriously cut by glass, metal, or shells in the sand or on seaside rocks; second- or third-degree sunburns; being stung by poisonous jelly fish; and automobile accidents driving to and from the beach.

Here are some questions you can research about tiger sharks in the library and on the Internet:

1. Why do you think tiger sharks prefer shallow reefs instead of open ocean to live in? What's near the reefs that the sharks want?

2. Does anything prey on sharks? What controls shark populations and keeps them from growing uncontrollably as the human population is currently doing?

Additional Reading

Here are references for information about sharks and coastal reef ecosystems. See your librarian for additional titles available at your local library.

Arnold, Caroline. *Watch Out for Sharks!* New York: Clarion Books, 1991.

Barrett, Norman. *Sharks*. New York: Franklin Watts, 1989.

Berger, Gilda. *Sharks*. Garden City, NY: Doubleday, 1987.

Blassingame, Wyatt. *Wonders of Sharks*. New York: Dodd, Mead, 1984.

Blumberg, Rhoda. *Sharks*. New York: Franklin Watts, 1976.

Budker, Paul. *The Life of Sharks*. New York: Columbia University Press, 1971.

Bunting, Eve. *The Sea World Book of Sharks*. San Diego, CA: Sea World Press, 1979.

Carrick, Carol. *Sand Tiger Shark*. New York: Seabury Press, 1977.

Cerullo, Mary. *Sharks: Challengers of the Deep*. New York: Cobblehill Books, 1993.

Cole, Joanna. *Hungry, Hungry Shark*. New York: Random House, 1986.

Cook, Joseph. *The Nightmare World of the Shark*. New York: Dodd, Mead, 1978.

Copps, Dale. *Savage Survivor: 300 Million Years of the Shark*. Milwaukee, WI: Westwind Press, 1976.

Coupe, Sheena. *Sharks*. New York: Facts on File, 1990.

Ellis, Richard. *The Book of Sharks*. New York: Grossett & Dunlap, 1976.

———. *Monsters of the Sea*. New York: Alfred A. Knopf, 1994.

Fletcher, Alan. *Fishes Dangerous to Man*. Reading, PA: Addison-Wesley, 1969.

Freedman, Russell. *Sharks*. New York: Holiday House, 1985.

Gibbons, Gail. *Sharks*. New York: Holiday House, 1992.

Gourley, Catherine. *Sharks!: True Stories and Legends*. Brookfield, CT: Millbrook Press, 1996.

Helm, Thomas. *Dangerous Sea Creatures*. New York: Funk & Wagnalls, 1976.

Langley, Andrew. *The World of Sharks*. New York: Bookwright Press, 1988.

Lawrence, R. *Shark!: Nature's Masterpiece*. Shelburne, VT: Chapters Publications, 1994.

MacQuitty, Miranda. *Shark*. New York: Alfred A. Knopf, 1992.

Maestro, Betsy. *A Sea Full of Sharks*. New York: Scholastic, 1990.

Markle, Sandra. *Outside and Inside Sharks*. New York: Atheneum Books for Young Readers, 1996.

McGovern, Ann. *Sharks*. New York: Four Winds Press, 1976.

Michael, Scott. *Reef Sharks of the World*. Monterey, CA: Challengers Books, 1993.

Perrine, Doug. *Sharks*. Stillwater, MN: Voyageur Press, 1995.

Robson, Denny. *Sharks*. New York: Gloucester Press, 1992.

Romashko, Sandra. *Shark: Lord of the Sea*. Miami, FL: Windward Press, 1987.

Sattler, Helen. *Sharks: The Super-Fish*. New York: Lothrop, Lee & Shepard, 1986.

Server, Lee. *Sharks*. New York: Gallery Books, 1990.

Steel, Rodney. *Sharks of the World*. New York: Facts on File, 1985.

Wexo, John. *Sharks*. Mankato, MN: Creative Education, 1989.

Feeding Frenzy

Piranhas of South America

At a Glance

We have all heard of piranhas. The word *piranha*, like *shark*, has wormed its way into our common speech as a way to describe a person as dangerous, as one who feeds off other people without regard to the damage or injury caused.

Thoughts of the fish, piranha, bring mental images of a huge mouth of razor-sharp teeth and a hungry body that will gobble up anything that touches the water.

The truth is somewhat different. Piranhas are a small, South American freshwater fish. They rarely grow to over a foot long and have round, flat bodies. They actually have small mouths and can only nibble a thimbleful at a time when they eat. But inside those petite mouths, piranhas have scalpel-sharp teeth and strong jaws that can easily slice through bone.

During the wet season, when rivers flow deep and are rich in food, piranhas aren't dangerous to anything as large as a human, unless that human is injured and trails blood into the water. During the wet season children regularly swim and play in the rivers where piranhas lurk.

But in the South American dry season, rivers shrink, and piranhas are trapped in huge schools of hundreds or even thousands of fish. Food is scarce. During the dry season, beware. At that time, all the stories of vicious piranha attacks are true.

"Feeding Frenzy"

Three boys stood on the bank of a thin, meandering tributary of the Orinoco River as it snaked its way deep inside the jungle flood plain of Venezuela, South America. One boy, the youngest, sat back a few feet on a thick root outcropping, intently watching the other two. These two stood at the river's edge, a stream really, no more than 10 feet across. Their dark-brown skin glistened in the splashes of sunlight that shown down along the river bank. Their straight, black hair flopped over their foreheads and was cut straight around the back as if an upside-down bowl had been placed on their heads when it was cut.

The boys were fishing. They used no poles, just thin fishing lines played out directly through their fingers. Their bare toes curled around roots, vines, and small rocks for a good grip, so they wouldn't be jerked off their feet if they got a strike.

"I will catch a fat bass fish," smiled one of the boys, tugging lightly on his line to make his lure hop through the water and look more attractive.

"I will catch a monster, wide-mouth catfish!" bragged the second. "My fish will be so big it will feed half our village."

"I will catch three big piranhas," replied the first, trying to outdo his friend. "Then father can use their teeth for his new wood-cutting saw."

The second boy laughed. "You can't catch a piranha. It would bite through your line." Then he bared his long, white teeth, clicked them up and down, and added, "And probably bite off your fingers and nose, too."

Both older boys laughed. But the youngest one shuddered and peered down at the dark green waters, sluggishly flowing around

From *Close Encounters with Deadly Dangers.* © 1998 Kendall Haven. Libraries Unlimited. (800) 237-6124.

thick clumps of floating water plants. "Do you really think there are piranhas here?"

The dozen species of piranhas are freshwater fish of South America. They would be just another small game fish (about one foot long and weighing two or three pounds) except for three unique characteristics. First, piranhas' teeth are sharper than a surgeon's scalpel, with strong jaw muscles to back them up. Second, they gather in vast schools, called shoals, of thousands of piranhas. Third, they are bold, aggressive fish and, when hungry, will attack *anything* that enters the water.

"I'm not afraid of piranhas," bragged the second boy. "I even swim with piranhas."

"Maybe in the wet season," said the first, again lightly tugging his line. "But this is near the end of the dry season. Food in the river is scarce for the fish. Water levels have dropped low, so the piranhas are bunched together too tightly."

"So?"

"So, being hungry and crowded makes piranhas crazy. They'll attack anything. Besides, the females may have already laid their eggs."

"So?" repeated the second boy.

"So, the males *guard* the eggs and will attack anything that comes near. You go in the water now and you'll come out a skeleton!"

The youngest boy trembled and his eyes grew wide as he stared at the quiet stream. "You think piranhas are down there waiting to attack us?"

The older boys lunged toward the youngest, dragging their lines through the water. "Maybe we'll throw you in and find out!"

The youngest boy screamed in fright. The older ones laughed.

Then they froze, listening. They heard the crunching and crackling of something walking through the underbrush across the stream. Instinctively, all three crouched low, holding still, watching. The hands of the older boys crept toward their bows.

"There!" hissed one of the older boys. "A capybara."

"If we catch a capybara," said the other. "We'll feed the whole village and be heroes."

Adult capybara, the world's largest rodents, which live only in the South American rain forests, often grow to over 100 pounds and

From *Close Encounters with Deadly Dangers.* © 1998 Kendall Haven. Libraries Unlimited. (800) 237-6124.

make for a delicious feast. This one was a hefty specimen and made the boys' eyes glisten with excitement.

"How can we catch it?" whispered the youngest boy. "It's on the other side of the river."

"We'll swim over very quietly and shoot it," answered the second boy, gently shaking his bow.

"There might be piranhas in the river," said the first boy.

"I'm not going in there," agreed the youngest.

"But I want the capybara!" hissed the second, the oldest of the three boys.

After a long pause while they watched the capybara shuffle its way through the dense underbrush near the opposite shore, the first boy said, "We'll have to test the water to see if it's safe."

"How?" asked the youngest.

"Splash in the water with a stick."

"Won't that scare the piranhas away?"

"Piranhas are very curious and have excellent hearing. If they're around, they'll come to investigate any unusual sound or vibration."

"No splashing," demanded the second boy. "The noise will scare the capybara away. Use a different test."

The first boy thought for a moment. "We'll drip blood onto a piece of breadfruit and drop it in the water."

The youngest boy giggled. "Fish don't eat fruit."

"Piranhas will. Piranhas eat anything, even other piranhas, especially if they smell blood. It makes them go crazy."

Both boys hauled in their fishing lines. The first used his hook to prick a small hole in his finger. He squeezed out five drops of blood onto a piece of breadfruit.

All three boys held their breath and stared as the fruit landed quietly on the calm surface of the water.

As it began to sink, small ripples criss-crossed on the surface. Suddenly the surface boiled as a frenzy of fins, tails, and blunt-nosed heads dove at the fruit. In the wink of an eye, the breadfruit was gone. The surface of the water returned to calm.

The boys panted for breath, their hearts pounding.

"Piranhas!" whispered the youngest.

From *Close Encounters with Deadly Dangers.* © 1998 Kendall Haven. Libraries Unlimited. (800) 237-6124.

"I don't think so," said the second boy. "Catfish sometimes eat breadfruit."

"Those were no catfish," insisted the first boy. "I saw the bodies, round and thin and about one foot long. Gold, white, and black markings on the back, and bright red underneath. Those were red-bellied piranhas, the most fierce of all!"

"But we *have* to cross to catch the capybara," argued the second boy. "Maybe these piranhas aren't hungry and will let us swim across."

The first boy gulped. "There's only one way to find out. Someone has to stick his finger in the water."

Both older boys turned to the youngest. "Stick your finger down in there."

He shrank back in horror. "No!"

"Don't you want to grow up to be a brave hunter?"

"No."

"I'll do it," huffed the oldest boy. "But then *I* get all the credit for catching the capybara."

"You can have it," whispered the youngest boy. "I'm not touching that water."

Trembling, the oldest boy inched forward as if the water itself would leap up and grab him. He stopped at the river's edge, staring at the peaceful green water and its soft reflection of the clear, blue sky above.

Shading his eyes he tried to peer past the water's surface to see what evil terrors lurked just below.

"Go ahead. Stir your finger around in the water."

He stretched out one trembling finger, pausing several inches above the water. Then his hand darted forward, brushed the surface for one micro-second, and jerked back. "It's safe," he triumphantly announced.

"That doesn't count. You have to *really* stick the finger down in there."

His face tight with fear, the oldest boy jammed his finger into the water and quickly stirred. The other two boys stared over his shoulder, their mouths dropped open.

From *Close Encounters with Deadly Dangers.* © 1998 Kendall Haven. Libraries Unlimited. (800) 237-6124.

Then the boy screamed and yanked back his finger. A small, neat chunk had been nipped off the end and blood already trickled down his wet hand into the water. The surface boiled as countless piranhas dove and pushed to find the source of the blood.

"Oww! My hand! He bit it off!" wailed the boy, shaking his sore finger.

"It's not a bad bite," said the first boy, holding the oldest one's hand still to examine the wound. "Put pressure on it and it'll stop bleeding in a minute."

Piranhas have small mouths, with a single row of triangular-shaped teeth with razor-sharp edges and needle-sharp points. They can only eat a thimbleful in each bite. But piranhas' jaws are strong enough to bite through bone or wood. One piranha can't do much damage to a large mammal, but when they hunt in shoals of over a thousand, they can devour an entire horse carcass in several minutes.

"Look at the women in our village," said the first boy, helping to wrap the injured fingertip, cut as neatly as if the fish had used a surgeon's scalpel. "They are all missing toes and fingertips from piranha bites while they washed clothes and gathered water for us to drink and cook with."

"We might as well go home," groused the oldest boy. "The capybara ran off when I yelled and we didn't catch any fish."

"Don't blame me," said the youngest boy. "I wasn't going to let piranhas eat me up!"

Then all three boys froze as a great crashing across the stream signaled a wildly running animal. The capybara burst back through the vines and underbrush at a frantic sprint, ears pressed back against its head, eyes wide with fright. Behind it a snarling roar broke like a thunderclap across the stream and rumbled like echoing thunder through the jungle.

"A panther," whispered the boys as they snatched their bows and dove for cover.

Desperately trying to escape from the panther, the capybara hurled itself off the river bank, leaping far out over the water. Its legs churned as if to swim through the air to the far side of the stream.

The panther, sleek, black, and pure muscled power, blasted through the shrubs, eyes and long fangs gleaming in the pools of sunlight. One step behind the capybara, the panther leapt like a rippling surge of fury after its prey.

From *Close Encounters with Deadly Dangers*. © 1998 Kendall Haven. Libraries Unlimited. (800) 237-6124.

In mid-air the cat's outstretched claws locked onto the capybara's back. Its snarling mouth swept down for a killing bite at the neck as they gracefully arched over the water.

Locked together, both animals crashed into the middle of the river with a great splash that soaked the boys as they watched from their hiding place behind a tree on the near bank. They heard the desperate squeals of the rodent as its head momentarily bobbed back to the surface. They heard the panther's roar of triumph turn into wild cries of rage and pain as it struggled to keep its head above water.

The water boiled into a white, frothing madness around the two animals, sounding like a thousand paddle wheels beating on its surface. Only the angry shrieks of the panther pierced through the dull roar of the piranhas' feeding frenzy.

The boys were too transfixed to blink. They were too startled to breathe. One second 100 pounds of capybara and 200 pounds of snarling black fury hurtled straight toward them. The next, both animals were swallowed by a boiling cauldron of death in the river, looking like the bubbling pot of some evil sorcerer.

In under four minutes the water calmed. Capybara and panther skeletons floated on the surface, picked white and clean.

Still staring wide eyed at the deadly stream, all three boys stumbled, trembling, back toward the safety of their village in awe-struck silence. There would be no more challenge of the mighty piranhas this day. Piranhas ruled the river and the boys would not test them again.

Thinking About This Ecosystem

Piranhas live in South American rivers and lakes. Are these bodies of water separate ecosystems? (*No. They are specific habitats within a larger ecosystem, the tropical rain forest ecosystem.*)

What is the difference between a habitat and an ecosystem? (*A habitat refers either to the place or region inhabited by a specific animal or plant, or to a specific and unique region within a larger system. Thus, a river is a specific and unique part of the rain forest, but is not a separate system from the rest of the rain forest. An ecosystem is an enclosed and separate system made up of a biological community [flora and fauna] and its non-living surroundings.*)

What plants grow in these river habitats to support the rest of the food chain? (*Algae, moss, grass, weeds, reeds, lilies, cattails, and many other plants grow in rivers and lakes, depending on the depth of water and on the speed of the current.*)

From *Close Encounters with Deadly Dangers.* © 1998 Kendall Haven. Libraries Unlimited. (800) 237-6124.

What predators are at the top of the food chain for a South American river habitat? How many of these actually live outside the habitat? (*Besides the various fish species, including piranhas, catfish, bass, etc., fish are preyed upon by birds, man, several jungle mammals—panthers, for example—and by amphibians, such as anacondas and caimans.*) Can you make a list of the species that depend on fish in the South American rain forest ecosystem?

South American rain forests have wet and dry seasons. See if you can find information about how these two seasons affect the plants and animals living in this ecosystem.

Thinking About This Predator

The name *piranha* comes from a South American tribal language and means "scissors fish." Piranhas live from two to five years and range throughout the freshwater systems of South America: rivers, streams, lagoons, and lakes. A fast fish with powerful tail muscles and small scales, there are over 30 different species of piranhas. Only a few are dangerous to large mammals. The red-bellied and black (both mentioned in this story) are the two most ferocious and dangerous species.

Piranhas are a very social fish, often traveling in shoals of over a thousand. Most active and prone to feed during the day, piranhas' main dietary targets are large insects, shrimp, fish, birds, rodents, mammals, and fruit. But when hungry, piranhas will eat almost anything.

Piranhas are not a top predator of their ecosystem. They are routinely hunted by large-mouth catfish, caimans, river dolphins, otters, wading birds, and humans. Piranhas are a very tasty and popular eating fish in South America.

Piranhas hunt with the same strategy that African lions use. They sneak up on and surround their prey, then one piranha rushes in to scatter the target species while the others wait to attack individuals as they scatter. No other predator fish uses this group attack strategy.

Here are some questions you can research about piranhas in the library and on the Internet:

1. Why do you think piranhas prefer to live in large schools, or shoals, instead of in small groups that would be easier to feed? How does social cooperation help piranhas?

2. Would having such sharp teeth be as important if piranhas ate only small fish they could gulp down in one bite? Do you think sharp teeth, small mouths, and group feeding are all related? Did they evolve together?

Additional Reading

Here are references for information about piranhas and the South American river ecosystem. See your librarian for additional titles available at your local library.

Cousteau, Jacques. *Jacques Cousteau's Amazon Journey.* New York: H. N. Abrams, 1984.

Gilliland, Judith. *River.* New York: Clarion Books, 1993.

Goulding, Michael. *Floods of Fortune: Ecology and Economy Along the Amazon.* New York: Columbia University Press, 1996.

Grossman, Susan. *Piranhas.* New York: Dillon Press, 1994.

———. *Piranhas.* New York: Silver Burdett, 1996.

MacGreagh, Gordon. *White Water and Black.* Chicago: University of Chicago Press, 1985.

McAuliffe, Emily. *Piranhas.* New York: Capstone Press, 1997.

McConnell, Rosemary. *The Amazon.* Morristown, NJ: Wayland, 1978.

O'Hanlon, Redmond. *In Trouble Again: A Journey Between the Orinoco and the Amazon.* New York: Atlantic Monthly Press, 1989.

Quinn, John. *Piranhas: Fact and Fiction.* Neptune City, NJ: T. H. F. Publications, 1992.

Schreider, Helen. *Exploring the Amazon.* Washington, DC: National Geographic Society, 1970.

Wallace, Alfred. *A Narrative of Travels on the Amazon and Rio Negro.* New York: Haskell House, 1969.

Squeeze Play

Anacondas of South America

At a Glance

Snakes have always fascinated humans. They have no arms, legs, wings, or feet. A snake is just a long, slick tube of a body with a head and mouth at one end and a tapered tail at the other. Snakes don't walk, crawl, hop, talk, or fly. They *slither*, silent and unseen through the grass. They are so different from us that they seem to be evil and sinister.

Big also fascinates humans. We are drawn toward a tyrannosaurus more than to a tiny compsognathus, to an elephant more than to an armadillo. Combine these two fascinations (big and snake), and you have one of the greatest fascinations of all: an anaconda. An anaconda is the biggest snake that has ever lived on earth. Anacondas have been measured at over 40 feet long with bodies 26 inches around. Specimens have been reported at up to 60 feet in length. That is a big snake!

Anacondas live deep in the tropical rain forests of South America, where they are the undisputed kings. Their remoteness makes them even more fascinating. Anacondas (as well as crocodiles and hippos) are included in the aquatic ecosystem section since their primary food sources come from that ecosystem.

"Squeeze Play"

High above, the rain ended. Sunlight streamed through the thinning clouds. Air hung thick and hazy over the forest. Birds in this top-most layer of the jungle chirped their welcome to the yellow light and hazy blue of the sky. Butterflies flitted their brilliant colors through the canopy.

The top canopy of leaves and thin branches spread out like a blanket more than 120 feet above the ground as far as the eye could see, a sea of green covering the world of the tropical rain forest below. This particular patch of rainforest canopy lay 490 miles up the Amazon River from the Brazilian city of Manous and 25 miles up a meandering tributary to the southwest. It was the heart of the Brazilian rain forest, a spot few humans had ever touched, an undisturbed place that had lived by the cycles of wet and dry in the tropical heat for hundreds of thousands of years.

Below this canopy, howler monkeys swung through the branches and cried for an end to the rain. Drops still dripped from the top canopy into the branches below as thick and hard as when it was raining. Toucans and parrots screeched for an end to the dripping wet.

Far below, in the dim, shadowy world on the ground, the rain would not end for over an hour as the drops worked their way down through the layers of branches one by one. Direct sunlight never penetrated to the floor of the jungle except as thin splashes of light landing in an occasional clearing along the banks of some river. Otherwise the jungle ground was a steamy world of perpetual twilight as light sifted through the layers of branches and leaves above.

There were separate worlds here in the rain forest, stacked on top of each other: One on the ground, one in the lower branches, and one in the high top of the dense green canopy.

From *Close Encounters with Deadly Dangers*. © 1998 Kendall Haven. Libraries Unlimited. (800) 237-6124.

The top world was made up of blue sky and green leaves and filled with things that flew and flitted. The bottom world was filled with green water, brown mud and tree trunks, gray-green bushes and sparse grass, and muggy heat held in by the trees above. Creatures down here were bigger and heavier than above, and relied on arms, legs, and fins instead of wings.

Each world had its own rules, climate, and rulers.

In the lower world a ruler began to stir. The first rumblings of hunger made her wake, made her shift in her coiled perch on a wide branch. She was a snake, and as a full-grown adult no animal dared challenge her. Two hundred and ninety pounds of muscle, 29 feet from nose to tail, she was an anaconda, the biggest of all the great snakes. At 23 inches around, she was thicker than many people's waists.

As a youth of only four or five feet long she had faced enemies and dangers. Eagles and other birds of prey, caimans (small South American cousins of the alligator), jaguars, and even wild boars could feast on a young anaconda. But she had survived the trials of youth. Now, five years later, her great size made her the queen of all the lands she touched.

Lounging on a wide branch, the anaconda feared nothing. If this were the dry season, even a mighty anaconda would avoid wide pools, where vast schools of starving piranhas, trapped by receding river levels, would attack and devour anything foolish enough to enter. But this was the middle of the rainy season. As one rain ended, heat turned puddles into steam. Steam turned the air into a sauna. Only the next rain cleared the steamy heat away by replacing it with a new flood of rain drops. In the rainy season, the air was always filled with water, the ground was always wet. These were the conditions an anaconda liked best.

Now hunger made her stir. She hadn't eaten since she devoured several catfish three days before. She preferred smaller meals like that, because they left her less lethargic afterwards. After a big meal she was often unable to move for several days. Even the queen had to be wary.

Thick as a tree trunk and colored dark olive green with wide blotches of black, the anaconda lowered her head toward the ground eight feet below, her long body slowly uncoiling along the branch

From *Close Encounters with Deadly Dangers.* © 1998 Kendall Haven. Libraries Unlimited. (800) 237-6124.

above. Her scaly skin glistened in the dim light, giving her the appearance of being wet and slimy, although she was really dry and smooth.

The anaconda twisted her head left and right in mid-air flicking her tongue in and out, sampling, tasting the faint chemical smells in the air.

She had limited mental ability to remember past trails and hunting spots. But she needed no memory to taste the direction to a nearby tributary and to sense that no prey were walking or crawling near the tree where she lounged. She would have to travel to hunt and eat tonight.

Occasionally she hunted from trees, dropping on her victims from above. Occasionally she prowled the ground, hoping to sneak up on unsuspecting prey. Most often she hunted from the water. On land she could move no faster than a human at a brisk walk, about five or six miles an hour. In the water she could propel her great mass at over 17 miles an hour, much faster than the fastest human swimmer.

Tonight she would hunt alone. She always hunted alone, and always at night. She had always lived alone, as do all anacondas, sleeping mostly on wide tree limbs.

Occasionally she had seen other anacondas, some smaller and some larger than herself, one great male measuring over 39 feet. Once she saw a gathering of anacondas, a mountain of twisting flesh of a dozen or more all intertwined in one great mound on the jungle floor.

But mostly she was alone. She hunted alone, ate alone, and rested alone. It was all she had ever known.

She reached the dirt floor of the rain forest and slithered in the direction of water. Her tail dropped from the tree with a slight plop behind her. The noise, though soft, seemed to echo along the quiet jungle floor. There was noise from birds, monkeys, buzzing insects, and tree frogs above. But the floor of the jungle itself was a very quiet place, a heavy, oppressive quiet that made intruders want to whisper instead of talking aloud.

The lack of noise didn't bother the anaconda. She had no ears to hear sounds, anyway. She had eyes, but was very near sighted. Vision was used only to coordinate the final strike, the moment of attack.

Even without good sight or hearing the anaconda was at no disadvantage. She easily sensed every detail of the world around her. She could feel the vibrations of approaching footsteps through her body's close contact with the ground. The chemical receptors on her

From *Close Encounters with Deadly Dangers*. © 1998 Kendall Haven. Libraries Unlimited. (800) 237-6124.

tongue, in her mouth, and in her nose were far more sensitive and powerful than any dog's nose. She could literally taste every nuance of the world around her by faint chemical scents released into the air.

She paused at the water's edge, blunt head nosing softly through bushes and thick tufts of tall grass, body stretched out along the mud behind her, longer than the length of two cars. Carefully, quietly, she raised her head, bobbing back and forth, tongue flicking in and out, sampling the air. With no lids her black eyes, cold and hard, stared ahead, never blinking.

Her chemical receptors detected something a little farther up the stream: A caiman. Yes, a large caiman lying still in the water ahead.

The caiman was hunting, hiding in some reeds in the shallows beside a wide clearing, waiting for some unsuspecting prey to approach the water for a drink. Five-feet long and weighing 90 pounds, the caiman was a fierce, quick fighter with strong legs and tail and powerful jaws. But it was no match for an adult anaconda attacking with the element of surprise.

An anaconda will devour whatever it finds. Deer, fish, large rodents, ducks, birds, even large turtles (shell and all) are swallowed whole.

But the caiman was a fighter with powerful jaws and sharp tearing teeth. It could inflict deadly wounds, so it would have to be approached carefully.

The anaconda slithered into the water. Only her nose, eyes, and tongue showed above the brown waterline. Her body undulated just below the surface. Quiet ripples spread out behind her head as she silently approached the prey.

The caiman, holding perfectly still with only its eyes above the water, concentrated on the land. It did not notice the soft water vibrations of approaching doom.

Patience, caution. Don't alarm the caiman too soon. Glide with the current. Give no warning. The anaconda inched ever closer. The caiman still waited in its ambush, unaware that it was an intended victim.

Now the anaconda drew close enough to "feel" the caiman through her heat-sensing organs, called *labial pits*. These organs next to the mouth produced an exact picture of the caiman's body in her brain by mapping its body temperature against the cooler background water and mud. Slowly, silently she gathered her great body

From *Close Encounters with Deadly Dangers*. © 1998 Kendall Haven. Libraries Unlimited. (800) 237-6124.

in tight S-curves like coils, like tight springs waiting to launch the ana-conda's head into a final assault.

Wait. . . . Wait. . . . Drift closer. . . .

With all the fury of a rampaging bull, the anaconda sprang for-ward, mouth gaping open, six rows of razor-sharp teeth gleaming in the dim light.

At the last second, the caiman became aware of her. Too late, it sprang forward to escape. Too late it spun to fend off the mighty at-tack. It knew it couldn't beat an adult anaconda, but it might block the attack and escape on land.

Before the caiman could hide its soft flanks behind open jaws, the anaconda struck, sinking 120 teeth into the caiman's hide, each over one inch long, each sharper than a shark's tooth. These deadly teeth were curved inward so the prey couldn't escape once the bite was set.

Anacondas do not bite like poisonous snakes, which bite to inject poison and then quickly spring back to avoid retaliation from their victims. Anacondas also do not bite like sharks, which try to rip flesh away one bite at a time.

Anacondas bite to hold on. Their bite does not kill. It keeps the prey from escaping while the anaconda loops its giant body around the victim in tight coils that will slowly squeeze the breath and life from the meal-to-be.

The caiman bellowed and twisted, trying to snap at the anacon-da's body, trying to throw the anaconda off like a bucking bronco.

But the anaconda had seen this maneuver before.

She pushed her coils hard against the shallow bottom of the stream to launch her head out of the water and into a rapid spin. Six feet of her own length rose from the water like a sea serpent. For a moment, she lifted the caiman clear of the water, its legs thrashing and its jaws snapping on empty air. She twisted her body to spin it through a complete circle, like a parent spinning a laughing child through the air.

As they crashed back to the muddy bank, the caiman was momentarily dazed and disoriented, unsure of which way lay escape and safety, which deadly danger. Mud splattered across nearby tree trunks. Sprays of foaming water blasted across the banks.

The anaconda knew her maneuver would create that moment of confusion. It always did. That one moment was all she needed.

From *Close Encounters with Deadly Dangers.* © 1998 Kendall Haven. Libraries Unlimited. (800) 237-6124.

Looping her upper body into a noose-like coil, she slipped it over the caiman's tail and along its body in three coils.

Only the jaws and tail of the caiman were visible as the anaconda began to squeeze.

Again the caiman bellowed, now from terror rather than anger. Again it spun in a wild attempt to escape, thrashing its tail, launching itself off one hind leg high into the air.

The anaconda rode with this leap like a seasoned rodeo rider. As they crashed back into the river a tidal wave of white spray drenched the far shore.

Anacondas do not crush their victims by squeezing these coils, splintering bones and pulverizing organs. They don't need to. Every time a frightened victim exhales, the anaconda squeezes just a little tighter, so that the prey can't expand its lungs to breathe in again. Soon the victim dies from lack of oxygen and can be leisurely swallowed and digested.

In a last desperate effort the caiman lunged for the anaconda's tail. But with a quick jerk of her head and a sharp squeeze of her coils, she moved it to safety. The caiman's jaws snapped on empty air for a final time.

Like ringing out a wet shirt, the anaconda's coils tightened, squeezing every drop of air from the caiman's lungs. Its jaws weakly opened and closed, but no air passed into the collapsed lungs beyond.

Long after the caiman had ceased to move or twitch the anaconda maintained its strangle hold. When she was finally convinced that life had ended, she relaxed her grip and lined up her mouth on the long axis of the caiman's inert body. Slowly she opened her jaws wider and wider, unhinging her lower jaw so that her mouth stretched wider than the circumference of her whole body.

Inch by inch she slithered up the caiman's body, absorbing it into her gullet as she went. It would take her over 20 minutes to swallow this meal, and almost three weeks to digest it. For that time she would rest, lying motionless in the wide lower branches of some great tree.

For those three weeks the jungle around her would breathe a little easier, animals would go about their daily routines feeling a little safer. But all too soon, the rumblings of hunger would stir deep inside her again, and terror would again prowl the floor of the rain forest.

From *Close Encounters with Deadly Dangers.* © 1998 Kendall Haven. Libraries Unlimited. (800) 237-6124.

Thinking About This Ecosystem

Anacondas live in the South American tropical rain forest. What makes a tropical rain forest ecosystem special and unique? (*Rain forests are the most productive—in amount of plant and animal biological mass produced each year—and the most diverse—having the greatest variety of plant and animal species—ecosystems on earth. They also contain an incredible number of unique plant and animal species, and produce a large portion of the world's oxygen.*)

Find the world's rain forests, record their location and size, and shade them in on a map. Which is the biggest? (*The Amazon rain forest.*) Which ones are being destroyed by human activity? Can you discover why they are being burned and cut down?

The anaconda is a top predator in the Amazon rain forest. If you lived there, how would you keep from being eaten by an anaconda? Are there weaknesses of an anaconda that you might turn into successful strategies for survival to protect yourself?

Thinking About This Predator

Anacondas are the world's largest snakes and are fierce predators, yet they are not poisonous. They do not use the weapon that most of the dangerous snakes of the world rely on. How have anacondas compensated for not being able to kill prey with poison? Do you think their lack of poison and their great size are related? How does one compensate for the other?

Anacondas live for up to 30 years and grow to over 30 feet, sometimes as long as 50 feet. How big is that? As a class project, build an anaconda out of cardboard or wire mesh and papier mâché. Make it a big anaconda, 35 feet long and 26 inches around (just over eight inches across) for most of its body, colored dark green to black. It would weigh 350 pounds. Use photographs as a guide to the look and texture of your snake. Make your anaconda full sized, but make it light enough to carry. Now that's a big snake!

Here are some questions you can research about anacondas in the library and on the Internet:

1. Anacondas are giant predators and live alone. Piranhas (predator fish in the same ecosystem) are small and live in large communal groups. Do you think there is a pattern here? Do bigger predators tend to live alone? Why? Can you find exceptions? In what situations do large predators live in groups?

2. Anacondas live in the hot tropical rain forest. Why do you think they don't live in the high mountains, the Southwest American deserts, or in Canada? What unique characteristics of the tropical rain forest are essential to an anaconda's survival?

3. How well do we know the full life cycle of an anaconda? What don't we know about this giant creature?

Additional Reading

Here are references for information about anacondas and the tropical rain forest ecosystem. See your librarian for additional titles available at your local library.

Bargar, Sherie. *Anacondas*. Vero Beach, FL: Rourke Enterprises, 1987.

Bender, Lionel. *Pythons and Boas*. New York: Gloucester Press, 1988.

Ethan, Eric. *Boas, Pythons, and Anacondas*. Milwaukee, WI: Gareth Stevens, 1995.

Fine, Edith. *The Python and Anaconda*. Mankato, MN: Crestwood House, 1988.

Frank, Weiner. *Boas and Other Non-Venomous Snakes*. Neptune City, NJ: T. H. F. Publications, 1990.

Mattison, Christopher. *Snakes of the World*. New York: Facts on File, 1986.

———. *The Encyclopedia of Snakes*. New York: Facts on File, 1995.

Parker, Hampton. *Snakes: A Natural History*. Ithaca, NY: Cornell University Press, 1977.

Pope, Clifford. *The Giant Snakes*. New York: Alfred A. Knopf, 1971.

Quiroga, Horicio. "The Return of the Anaconda." In *Tales from Argentina,* edited by Frank Waldo. New York: Farrar & Rinehart, 1940.

———. *The Decapitated Chicken and Other Stories*. Austin, TX: University of Texas Press, 1976.

Roberts, Mervin. *All About Boas and Other Snakes*. Neptune City, NJ: T. H. F. Publications, 1975.

A "Croc" of Jaws

Crocodiles of Central Africa

At a Glance

Crocodiles and alligators are cousins. Both are large, mostly aquatic reptiles. Both have the same basic body, tail, leg, and head shapes. Both have long mouths filled with rows of pointed, jagged teeth. Both are carnivores.

But there are differences. Crocodiles are bigger, the largest reptiles on earth. The snout of a crocodile is narrower and more pointed. They are more aggressive and quicker to attack.

In zoos, both alligators and crocodiles act like huge sluggards, lying around inert and are boring to watch. Yet they look ferocious, even lying quietly in the sun. They look mean and dangerous. Their long, curving mouths with pointed, scraggly teeth look designed to kill.

A crocodile may show a crooked smile, but everyone knows that smile can't be trusted. Crocodiles are ambushers, lying in wait, still as harmless logs in the water. Then they pounce. Their great jaws slam shut. Another victim is dragged under water and is gone.

Maybe crocodiles look dangerous to us, even when they are lying quietly in the sun, because they *are* dangerous, as dangerous as any big predator on earth.

"A 'Croc' of Jaws"

The sun inched over the distant eastern heights, yellow and hot. Shadows stabbed across the grassy plain, across herds of grazing wildebeests and antelopes, and across the winding river as it flowed on to the west.

The current of this meandering, unnamed river near Nairobi National Park in Kenya, Africa, flowed thick, brown, and lazy past steep banks of sandy dirt, thick clumps of bushes, clusters of acacia and taller sausage trees, and endless fields of waving savanna grasses, badly trampled at several places where the shallow slope of the bank created a natural watering spot.

Just below one of these popular watering spots the tip of a gray, submerged rock protruded above the water line, marking a shallow spot in the river. Or maybe it was one trim end of a sunken log nosed above the current, creating a rippling wake as the water trudged past.

It couldn't be a log; it blinked. Farther out in the stream lay a second pair of blinking eyes, eyes that had to be part of a very large creature.

Lily pads and Nile cabbage floated in thick clumps on the river's surface. Plover birds darted back and forth across these walkways on their long, stalk-like legs, searching for insects.

Overhead two eagles circled in search of fish lingering too near the surface. One looked down and screeched in anger. Any fish in the area would be on their guard, slinking past in the shadows and depths. From their vantage on high, the fish eagles could see why. A line of great crocodiles hung in the water, eyes blinking at the water line, tails softly beating to keep them motionless near the watering spot, watching, waiting.

These were Nile crocodiles, one of 14 separate species of crocodiles that inhabit tropical and subtropical regions worldwide. The biggest and most vicious of all crocodiles are the saltwater crocodiles that live from northern Australia up to India. These monsters reach 28 feet in length and weigh as much as 3,000 pounds.

From *Close Encounters with Deadly Dangers.* © 1998 Kendall Haven. Libraries Unlimited. (800) 237-6124.

The Nile crocodiles rarely reach 20 feet in length and weigh under 2,500 pounds. Still, even an average-sized Nile crocodile can bring down a full-grown lion if the croc attacks without being seen.

The eyes of one of the crocodiles silently slid toward shore. Slowly a long, triangular head rose above the water line like a surfacing submarine. The crocodile has no lips, so its 30 fearsome, cone-shaped teeth always stick out in full and terrifying view.

Next its back emerged, broad and flat, as water streamed off between long rows of thick horny bumps and plates. Its broad tail and stubby legs could be seen as the crocodile waddled onto the sandy shore. It opened its great jaws and uttered a long, low, rumbling growl that sounded as threatening as the crocodile looked.

This crocodile, an 18-foot giant, flopped onto its belly to bask in the warmth of the morning sun. Slowly other full-grown adults wandered onto shore near the first. Soon five monsters were lined up next to each other, like cars in a parking lot. Crocodiles, the only surviving members of the dinosaur family, do little hunting during the day. Rather, they use this time to soak in the sun's warmth. Being cold blooded, they need this heat to stay active through the night's hunting session.

This was early spring. Today would not be nearly as hot as the summer. The crocodiles would spend most of the day basking, soaking up as much solar radiation as possible. From the distance, a lion's throaty roar echoed across the river, celebrating the previous night's kill.

A smaller crocodile crawled out of the water onto a small sand bar away from the line of bigger crocodiles. The young croc, a male, warily eyed the line of bigger crocs before settling into the warm sun. Crocodiles will eat anything that flies, crawls, walks, or swims, if it comes near enough to grab. That includes younger or smaller crocodiles. In fact, adult crocs are one of the biggest predators of newborn and juvenile crocodiles. Every young crocodile knows that the slight upward curve of an adult crocodile's mouth may *look* like a friendly smile, but behind that smile lies a heartless killing machine.

Crocodiles measure about one foot long when hatched and grow about ten inches per year. The young crocodile on the sand bar was five years old and measured just over five feet from nose to tip of tail.

As the afternoon warmed, the line of crocodiles opened their mouths by raising their upper jaw, like a line of cars with their hoods propped up. They looked as though they were waiting for some foolish

From *Close Encounters with Deadly Dangers.* © 1998 Kendall Haven. Libraries Unlimited. (800) 237-6124.

animal to walk right in and become dinner. Actually, they were using the moist membranes of their great mouths and throats to radiate excess heat and keep from becoming too hot.

One of the crocs ambled into the shade of a bush to keep from overheating. Plover birds scampered around the crocodiles, pecking at leeches. Several walked right into gaping mouths to peck at debris trapped at the base of the great crocodile teeth.

As the sun dipped low toward the west and shadows raced eastward across the plain, the young male crocodile slid back into the water to hunt. Crocodiles change their diet as they grow. Hatchlings eat insects and frogs for their first year or two, then slowly change to a diet of fish. As they approach adulthood, crocodiles need bigger meals and switch to a diet of mostly mammals.

The young crocodile was planning his first mammal hunt. He had watched adults attack countless beasts at the watering spot. He was sure he knew the techniques and patterns for an attack. He was hungry to make his first mammal kill.

The young crocodile trod water among lily pads next to the water hole, waiting, watching, his eyes and nostrils above water but hidden by the thick lily pads. A family of elephants wandered down to drink and bathe. The young croc didn't dare attack even the infant elephant when it stuck its trunk into the river for a drink.

He had watched other crocodiles attack elephants. One was trampled to death by an enraged mother elephant. One was picked up by a bull elephant's trunk, shaken so hard its back snapped, and tossed into the high branches of an acacia tree, where its dead bones bleached white before they fell back to the ground.

No. He would not make his first attack on an elephant.

The sun set. An orange glow filled the western sky. A group of zebras nervously edged down the gentle slope of the watering spot. Zebras were the perfect target for his first catch!

Two zebras lowered their heads to drink. Others scanned the bushes and grass beyond for signs of predators.

It was time to attack. The young crocodile allowed the current to carry him forward, nearer and nearer, only eyes and nostrils above the water.

In the distance a hyena cried. It was answered by the nearer roar of a lion. All the zebras raised their heads to listen.

The young crocodile drifted ever closer.

From *Close Encounters with Deadly Dangers.* © 1998 Kendall Haven. Libraries Unlimited. (800) 237-6124.

One mid-sized zebra stood with both front hooves in the water. That one would be the crocodile's first kill.

He knew he must attack fast and hard to avoid being trampled. Spring forward, get a solid grip with one fierce snap of his jaws, flip the zebra off balance and into the water, then drag it under until it drowned. That was the classic crocodile attack pattern. That was his plan.

Drifting ever closer through the lily pads he could smell the zebras, even hear the buzzing of the flies that hovered around them.

The zebra gently dropped its head for another drink. This was the moment!

Racing forward on his webbed feet, driving forward with his powerful tail, the crocodile erupted like a deadly torpedo from the quiet river in an explosion of foaming water. His great upper jaw swung open.

He rammed into the zebra, colliding with its soft underbelly just behind its left front leg. He slammed his jaw shut, locking his teeth into the zebra's flank with amazing power and force. Water poured from his mouth as his jaws crashed shut. A cloud of hissing vapor blew from his nostrils like steam from a boiling kettle.

Zebra ribs cracked with a loud snap. Zebra skin was punctured and torn. Zebra blood flowed.

The zebra staggered and bellowed, but did not fall as it might have if attacked by a bigger crocodile.

With all his might the young crocodile threw his body into a violent spin to flip the zebra off its feet and into the water. Splashing water sprayed across the drinking spot. The other zebras fled to the safety of the top of the bank.

But the stricken zebra instinctively spread its legs for better balance. The crocodile's flip didn't work. Though flesh was torn and twisted from its chest, the zebra stayed on its feet.

Ears plastered back against its head, eyes wide and white with terror, the zebra bellowed a cry for help. Then it bucked in a desperate attempt to throw off the crocodile.

But the young croc's hold was good. His massive jaws locked onto muscle and bone. He flopped and shook as the zebra bucked, but he did not let go.

Now the struggle turned into a desperate tug-of-war. The crocodile's claws dug in. His tail thrashed in the shallow water. Again he tried to flip his body and throw the zebra off its feet.

From *Close Encounters with Deadly Dangers.* © 1998 Kendall Haven. Libraries Unlimited. (800) 237-6124.

Again the zebra resisted and stayed upright. Its hooves frantically beat and stomped on sand and dirt, pulling away from the deadly river.

The crocodile was losing the contest. Inch by inch he was being dragged out of the river. Though badly wounded, with its front leg painted red from flowing blood, the zebra slowly pulled the crocodile up the sloping bank.

This was not going right. The young croc had never seen a crocodile being dragged away before. Crocodiles were supposed to throw their victims savagely into the stream. Still refusing to let go, the crocodile was suddenly unsure of what he was supposed to do next.

A deep, throaty growl rumbled from a crocodile on the other side of the zebra. There was a great "thud," a deep shudder, and the zebra seemed to lift off the ground and bound sideways toward the young crocodile. The 18-foot monster had joined the hunt and had crashed into the zebra, locking onto its other side just in front of the rear leg.

Yelping in pain and surprise, the zebra's back legs collapsed. It sank onto its haunches.

Now a third adult raced forward to lock onto the zebra's shoulder, just above the young crocodile.

The young crocodile realized there was suddenly great danger here. First, he was on the bottom of a growing pile of massive adult crocodiles and a dying zebra. He could be crushed. Second, he was still small enough to be considered part of the feast by older crocodiles. If he held his grip and his ground, he would more likely *become* dinner than *get* dinner.

Reluctantly, the young crocodile released his hold and scurried back toward the river as one of the adults snapped fiercely at his hind leg.

From the safety of his sand bar the young croc bellowed his protest with all his might, a deep, threatening growl, as the three adult crocodiles savored his meal, *his* zebra, *his* first mammal catch.

Again he cried his frustration and rage. He was answered only by the distant roar of a hunting lion.

He didn't slide back into the water until the adults had completely devoured his prize. It had been a foolish attack. The zebra had been too big for him to handle. He had escaped what could have easily been his own destruction.

From *Close Encounters with Deadly Dangers*. © 1998 Kendall Haven. Libraries Unlimited. (800) 237-6124.

There were still plenty of fish in the river. He would grow. There would soon come another day and another hunt.

Thinking About This Ecosystem

Why don't other species just leave whenever they see a crocodile anywhere around? (*They need water, whether or not there are crocodiles present. Most, in fact almost all, of the animals who come to a river for a drink leave very much alive. It's like people and cars. We need and use cars, even though cars are dangerous and many people are killed in automobile accidents each year. But most of us aren't. We need them, we use them, and we "escape" just fine.*) Are there other elements of our lives and of our ecosystem that are inherently dangerous, but which we don't avoid because we benefit from them?

Besides crocodiles, what other predators do the animals in the African plains ecosystem have to worry about? Make a list of these predators and of the grazers and browsers who could fall prey to each. Are there animals in this ecosystem who *don't* need to worry about (fear) crocodiles? Make a list of these animals and why they don't fear crocs. (*Besides listing big animals such as adult elephants and hippos, remember to think of the very small members of the animal population of a savanna grass ecosystem.*)

Thinking About This Predator

Crocodiles hatch on shore from eggs. The mother croc protects and guides, or carries, her 12-inch-long hatchlings as far as the water. Then they are on their own. The sex of these hatchlings is determined by their incubation temperature. Eggs maintained at temperatures below 85 degrees Fahrenheit develop as males. Those incubated at above 95 degrees Fahrenheit turn into females. Between those temperatures, they can go either way.

The word *crocodile* comes from the Greek word *krokodilos*, which means "lizard." The name of the crocs' close cousin, the alligator, comes from the Spanish word for lizard, *"el lagarto."* Crocodiles and alligators are the only surviving members of the reptile family to which the dinosaurs belonged. It is easy to imagine crocodiles as part of the dinosaurs' world.

Crocodiles, who live up to 75 years, eat, on average, only 50 meals a year. How many do you eat? Of course, each of their meals may weigh 50 or 60 pounds. This story mentions the tremendous force of a crocodile's closing jaws. Their jaws exert 1,200 pounds of pressure per square inch while closing. How much pressure is that? An average human, standing on both feet, exerts a pressure of between two and three pounds per square inch on the floor below. If a 150-pound man balanced his entire weight on the tip of one

---

From *Close Encounters with Deadly Dangers*. © 1998 Kendall Haven. Libraries Unlimited. (800) 237-6124.

finger, he still wouldn't exert more than 300 pounds of pressure per square inch, less than one-quarter of what a crocodile's jaws exert!

Here are some questions you can research about crocodiles in the library and on the Internet:

1. Crocodiles allow plover birds to walk around and on them, and even into their mouths. Yet crocs never eat plover birds. This is one of the symbiotic relationships in nature. What do crocodiles do for plover birds? What do plover birds do for crocodiles?

2. Do you think crocs are part of an aquatic or terrestrial ecosystem? (*Actually both of these habitats are part of only one ecosystem, the African savanna grassland ecosystem. Crocodiles are amphibious and travel into both aquatic and terrestrial habitats within this ecosystem. What advantages do they gain from being amphibious?*)

3. Why do crocs congregate near watering holes? What else congregates there that the crocodiles need?

Additional Reading

Here are references for information about crocodiles. See your librarian for additional titles available at your local library.

Bender, Lionel. *Crocodiles and Alligators*. New York: Gloucester Press, 1988.

Brennan, Frank. *Reptiles*. New York: Macmillan, 1992.

Bright, Michael. *Crocodiles and Alligators*. New York: Gloucester Press, 1990.

George, Jean Craighead. *The Moon of the Alligators*. New York: HarperCollins, 1991.

Guggisberg, C. A. *Crocodiles: Their Natural History, Folklore, and Conservation*. Harrisburg, PA: Stackpole Books, 1982.

Neill, Wilfred. *The Last of the Ruling Reptiles*. New York: Columbia University Press, 1979.

Perry, Phyllis. *The Crocodilians: Reminders of the Age of Dinosaurs*. New York: Franklin Watts, 1997.

Ross, C., ed. *Crocodiles and Alligators*. New York: Facts on File, 1989.

Taylor, Dave. *The Alligator and the Everglades*. Toronto: Crabtree Publishing, 1990.

Tibbitts, Allison, and Alan Roocroft. *Crocodiles*. Mankato, MN: Capstone Press, 1992.

Zim, Herbert. *Alligators and Crocodiles*. New York: William Morrow, 1978.

Treacherous Tusks

Hippopotamuses of Central Africa

At a Glance

The name *hippopotamus* comes from ancient Greek and means "water horse." Humans have often thought of hippos as the ugliest creatures on earth. Their huge, round bodies, loose, pink skin, oversized, misshapen heads, scraggly hairs, and tall ears make them look comical and silly, anything but dangerous.

Hippos are the only non-predator deadly danger in this book. They are one of a few vegetarian species that willingly, aggressively attack humans. In fact, hippos in Africa kill more humans each year than lions, elephants, and the feared African buffalo combined. Far from the fat, waddling creatures they appear to be in zoos, hippos are fast, mean, and deadly.

49

"Treacherous Tusks"

His ears flicked back and forth to drive out the water that dribbled into them and to shake off a pesky fly. He snorted a great whooshing of air and water vapor. Then he breathed in, deep and contented. If those young males out on the fringe didn't try to move in on his territory, it would be a peaceful fall.

Satisfied, he sank under the blue-green river water and settled to the grassy bottom. Hippopotamuses are one of the few mammals that are naturally heavier than water. Unless they actively swim, they always sink. Maybe he'd nibble at the bottom grasses. But mostly, he would just sit and enjoy the next five minutes before he rose again to breathe.

The river was the Lomami River, running warm, wide, and shallow through Zaire in central Africa. Curving sandbars and twisting channels wove between the sloping banks. Great seas of grass and thickets of acacia trees lay beyond on both sides. The seasons swung from steamy hot during the rainy seasons to blistering hot during the long dry seasons. The fall rainy season was just beginning.

This male (bull) hippo, weighing almost four tons and measuring 14 feet nose to tail, was a ranking male in this herd of hippopotamuses, called a school, that had lived in this wide bend in the river for over a year. Fifteen females and as many calves clustered in a central pool, called a *creche*, along the north side of a sandbar. Scattered around this core, each male claimed his own small plot of river, called a *refuge*.

Ranking males staked out refuges near the females. Young males, just starting to fight their way up the social order, and weak old males stayed on the distant outskirts of the school.

The bull rose for a breath and twitched his ears to clear them as he again eyed the five-year-old males farther up river who had been roaring challenges to all senior males. Hippo sounds range from soft grunts, to coughing barks, to great throaty, honking roars that echo up and down the river. Roars were issued either as a challenge or a warning.

The bull decided to let the upstarts know how unwelcome they would be in the inner circle near the females and young. He stretched his great mouth open almost five feet from upper to lower lip, an

From *Close Encounters with Deadly Dangers*. © 1998 Kendall Haven. Libraries Unlimited. (800) 237-6124.

endless mass of bright-pink folds and squiggles of moist skin with a slithering tongue as long as a human arm and as thick as a human leg. A full-grown male hippo has the biggest mouth on earth except for whales. It's big enough for many humans to stand in. This bull hippo opened his great mouth and roared back. The sound carried for a mile across the grasses.

But it was not the sound itself that drove fear into creatures near the river. Fear was created by the teeth and tusks, the weapons in that great mouth. A hippo's curving tusks grow to three feet in length and end in lethal points. Long canine teeth and sharp incisors grow to 18 inches and criss-cross like scissors to cut through grass, branches, or flesh during a fight. Forty enormous teeth grind and pulverize anything that gets inside.

Satisfied with his warning, the bull decided to drift into the central creche and play with his son. Hippos love to play, especially with their young, until they mature (at three years for females and at four for males). Then they become just more adults competing for food and position within the community.

Hippos live in a matriarchal society. Even this great bull couldn't enter the creche area to play with his own six-month-old son without permission. As he slowly nosed toward them, two females, including his son's mother, grunted their approval, batted their tall ears, and eased aside to let him pass.

The hippo's son was practicing belly flops into the shallow water off a sandbar when the bull approached. They greeted each other with pretend bites and nuzzles, the father a mostly gray, great barrel of a body, bigger than a car, and his son a mostly pink, smaller barrel weighing only 600 pounds and measuring just five feet long.

With squeals and grunts of delight the calf scrambled to climb onto his father's back, stubby legs and hoof-like toenails splashing through the water and scratching his father's skin. The bull stooped low enough in the water to make sure his son would succeed. Once on top of his father's back, the calf tumbled off the far side, splashing into the river. Instantly he was back at his father's side, clamoring up for another somersaulting roll.

When the bull tired of this game, he roughly nosed his calf aside. The calf responded by opening his mouth, growling, and charging at his father's head. Practice fights would become the calf's all-consuming game as he grew. Once the calf turned four, the fights

From *Close Encounters with Deadly Dangers.* © 1998 Kendall Haven. Libraries Unlimited. (800) 237-6124.

would be real and would determine his success in the school, even his survival.

As father and son flopped, splashed, and rolled through their practice fight, one of the females bellowed. The game had grown too rough and had disturbed the peace of the creche. Two females turned on the bull, mouths yawning open, tusks slashing at the air. He quickly retreated to his refuge, having been driven out of the central area.

There was a bellowing and splashing commotion on the shore. A crocodile had lunged at another young hippo calf playing in the shallows. Its enraged mother sprinted back from the grassy bluff in a blur of stubby legs and massive body. A hippo can run at over 40 miles per hour, almost twice as fast as an Olympic sprinter. In less than five seconds the conflict was over. The crocodile had been crushed to death by 6,000 pounds of steamrolling fury before it could lock its teeth onto the calf. The croc's lifeless body lay deep in the mud where the tree-trunk thick legs had pounded it. Vultures began to circle overhead.

The bull grunted. The croc should have known better than to challenge a hippopotamus mother. No natural force in Africa can withstand an enraged female hippo.

A five-year-old male nosed into the bull's refuge, only its eyes, pointed ears, and nostrils above water.

Here it came: A challenge.

The bull yawned his great mouth wide open and bellowed a warning, but the young male did not retreat. He yawned his own mouth wide and returned a threatening roar.

This one is cocky and aggressive, thought the bull. *But he has no battle scars.*

The old bull's head, shoulders, and front legs were criss-crossed by deep, ragged scars from countless battles over the years. Each scar represented a lesson learned, a fighting trick observed and mastered. The lack of scars meant that this young buck had no experience, and should be easy to trick and defeat.

Again the bull's honking roar warned the intruder. But the young bull edged closer, mouth open and tusks slicing through the air as he swung his bulbous head.

The old bull edged backward until he knew he had better footing than the young intruder. The young bull continued to roar, and confidently swam forward into the heart of the old bull's refuge.

Then the old bull attacked. Eight thousand pounds of force behind three-foot tusks launched into an arc aimed at the intruder's neck. A tidal wave sprayed across the river as the old bull crashed through the water.

The young bull swung his head to meet the attack, but he was a fraction of a second too late. His tusks scraped across the old bull's shoulder, barely breaking the skin, while the old one's tusks sank into soft flesh.

The young bull staggered back, his shoulder gashed open through the thick fat layer that surrounds a hippo and into the muscle below. Now the old bull's tusks slashed sideways across the intruder's neck and jowls. Again the young bull staggered back as a three-foot gash opened in the skin of his neck.

The old bull dove under water to lash at the intruder's legs. The young bull ducked and met him. Their tusks and mouths crashed together with a smack that reverberated through the river.

Locked tusk to tusk and open mouth to open mouth, both bulls exploded through the surface, seeking to gain an upper hand. White spray splattered both banks and every hippo in the school as they watched. The old bull used his extra weight to muscle the intruder back out of his territory.

In full retreat, the young bull staggered onto a sandbar and collapsed. His wounds would take months to heal fully. The battle scars would last a lifetime. Next time this one would be wiser and not as easy to beat.

Through panting gasps for breath, the old bull roared his declaration of victory. He had only one small gash to heal and add to his collection of battle scars. The fight had gone better than he had expected. Other young males would press their challenges for status and territory elsewhere around the school, but his ranking would probably go untested for the rest of the season. None of the young bulls would dare risk the injuries.

The sun dipped toward the western horizon in a fuzzy red ball, shimmering through the heat waves rolling off the grassy plain. It cast a pink and orange glow across the water. As if the color change were a traffic signal, many of the hippos swam toward shore. Hippos can walk on the bottom at about eight miles per hour, and swim at 12.

From *Close Encounters with Deadly Dangers.* © 1998 Kendall Haven. Libraries Unlimited. (800) 237-6124.

One by one enormous hippo bodies lumbered onto shore to feed on the sweet grasses. Their thick, stubby legs seemed barely long enough to keep their bellies from dragging on the ground.

Hippo skin ranges from pink to dark gray and is almost hairless. Though thick and tough, hippo skin is actually quite sensitive and would quickly sunburn and crack if hippos didn't stay in the water for most of the day. During the day they graze on floating and bottom river plants. At night they feast on the waving fields of grass on shore.

The bull decided to stay in his river refuge and rest after his battle. He would feed longer tomorrow night.

In the shadowed twilight he heard rhythmic splashing and voices upriver, drifting slowly closer.

"How far before we camp?"

"We have to reach a safe spot in the river first."

"This looks safe enough to me."

"That is why I am the guide and you are the tourist."

"Are there crocodiles here? Lions? Piranha?"

"Piranha are only in South America. Here in Africa we have hippopotamuses."

The bull snorted in disgust. It was humans. Hippos hate humans, their only enemy. Six humans in an inflatable boat—four tourists with cameras, two guides with paddles and rifles—floated on a river safari.

The tourists laughed. "Hippos are lazy, fat, ugly, and slow. We paid to see some *real* dangers."

The guides had grown tense and wary. "Traveling this stretch of river at night is both smart and foolish. Smart, because many of the hippos are on shore feeding. Foolish, because in the dark we can't see refuges and the creche to avoid."

The bull sank low in the water. If this invader boat entered his refuge, he would attack.

The guides pulled in their oars, nervously straining to hear a telltale sound, swirling flashlight beams across the water, hoping to light up any danger.

"Did you hear bubbles? Soft breathing?"

Now the tourists grew frightened as well. "Yes. Bubbles. What *was* it?"

From *Close Encounters with Deadly Dangers.* © 1998 Kendall Haven. Libraries Unlimited. (800) 237-6124.

"Shhh!" The hand of one guide crept toward his rifle. He whispered, "This is bad, very bad I think. I fear you will get to see your deadly danger."

Complete silence reigned on the river as the boat drifted past a sandbar and around a wide bend. All six inside hunched low in the boat, staring wide-eyed into the black waters surrounding them.

Again the bubbles, closer this time.

"This side!" cried one guide.

"No. It came from over *here!*" shouted the other. Flashlight beams raced across empty, black water.

As if out of a nightmare, a great head, seemingly big enough to swallow the entire boat erupted from the water beside the travelers. The old bull's yellow, deadly tusks, each longer than a baseball bat, gleamed in the flashlight beams and whistled as they sliced through the air. His monstrous head seemed to fill the sky next to the boat. His roar blasted across the six terrified people like a gale.

Screams were frozen in the travelers' throats as the great mouth lifted their boat in the air like a toy. Sharp incisors sliced through the rubber siding, exploding two of the inflatable sections with deafening bangs!

The roar seemed to reverberate forever as the people and their broken boat were tossed through the air, tumbling over and over before they crashed into the water.

Now other roars joined the first, roars of warning from every side.

"Hippos!" screamed one guide. "Swim for the sandbar."

"My camera!" cried one tourist.

"Forget the camera. Save your life!"

"Shoot it!" cried another.

"My rifle went over the side," answered a guide. "Swim and pray!"

With the invaders driven out of his territory, splashing through the water after their boat and possessions, the great bull settled back low into the water. His four thick toes kneaded the soft mud of the river's bottom. This was shaping up to be a good fall indeed.

———

From *Close Encounters with Deadly Dangers*. © 1998 Kendall Haven. Libraries Unlimited. (800) 237-6124.

Thinking About This Ecosystem

Hippos live in African rivers and lakes. They feed both in the water and, at night, on land. On land they eat grasses. What do they eat during the day in the rivers? (*Bottom grass and floating plants.*) In this way, what services do hippos provide for other members of the river and lake ecosystem? (*They keep plants from choking waterways and, by eating great masses of plants, keep decaying plants from using up precious oxygen in the water, which fish need to survive.*)

Are other African animals afraid of the hippopotamus? Why or why not? (*No, they aren't. Hippos are herbivores, not meat-eating predators, and do not attack other animals. They fight only to defend themselves, their families, and their territories.*)

Thinking About This Predator

Hippopotamuses are one of the few herbivores in the world that are seriously dangerous to humans and other animals. Can you name others? (*The list includes many large animals, such as elephants and buffalo. Two in particular, like the hippo, are fiercely territorial, aggressive, and quick to fight: the rhinoceros in Africa, and the moose in North America.*)

Hippopotamuses live all their 30-year lives in a very territorially oriented society. Are most animals territorial? Are predators more territorial than browsers and grazers? (*Virtually all predators are somewhat territorial. They have to claim and defend a territory so that all the prey that wander into it will be theirs to attack. Only a few herbivores are territorial, including the hippopotamus. Most herbivores have to wander over vast spaces in search of ample water and food supplies.*)

Are there predators who prey on juvenile hippos? (*Yes. All major African predators will do so if they have the opportunity.*) Are there predators who attack adult hippos? (*Generally, no. Hippos are too big to attack safely. It would be difficult, if not impossible, for most predators to bring down an adult hippo.*) How do hippos defend themselves? (*Hippos are armed with fierce tusks to maim any attacker. If a hippo were sick, badly wounded, or old and weak, however, it would be vulnerable.*)

Here are some questions you can research about hippopotamuses in the library and on the Internet:

1. Why are hippopotamuses so dangerous to man?

2. Hippopotamuses live in a physically structured society. Females and young are in the middle, while males spread out in their private plots all around. Why do they live like this? Why not just wander wherever they want? What advantage do they gain from keeping big males apart in their own spaces? What advantage do they gain from keeping all the females and young in the middle of this wide ring of males?

Additional Reading

Here are references for information about hippopotamuses and river ecosystems. See your librarian for additional titles available at your local library.

Arnold, Caroline. *Hippo*. New York: Morrow Junior Books, 1989.

Burst, Beth. *Hippos*. Mankato, MN: Creative Education, 1991.

Denis-Hout, Christine. *The Hippopotamus (Animal Close-Ups)*. Boston: Charlesbridge Publishing, 1994.

Du Chaillu, Paul. *Explorations and Adventures in Equatorial Africa*. New York: Negro Universities Press, 1969.

Lasher, Faith. *Hubert Hippo's World*. Chicago: Childrens Press, 1981.

Lavine, Sigmund. *Wonders of Hippos*. New York: Dodd, Mead, 1983.

Pouyanne, Therese. *Hippo*. New York: Rowke Book, 1983.

Trevisick, Charles. *Hippos*. Milwaukee, WI: Raintree Children's Books, 1980.

Weyo, John. *Hippo*. Mankato, MN: Creative Education, 1991.

Stories
from
Terrestrial
Ecosystems

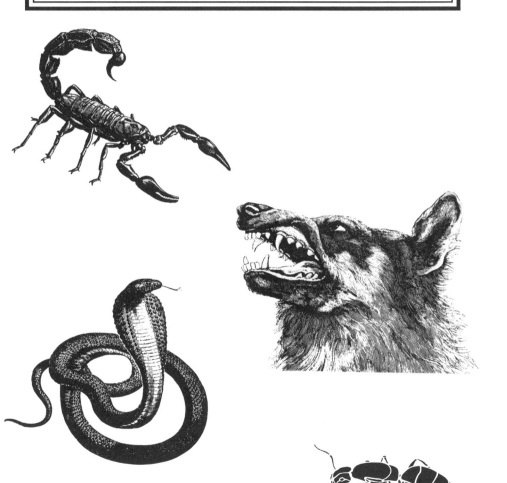

Death by Numbers

Army Ants of South America

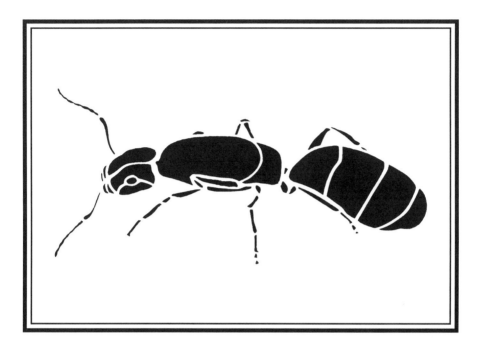

At a Glance

Ants seem to be harmless. Oh, they can be bothersome pests, but even biting red ants, which leave itching welts where they bite, are far from dangerous.

But what if a thousand ants, or a hundred thousand, or an army of 30 million hungry, meat-eating ants attached? Would this thick sea of carnivorous insects extending 200 yards across and half a mile long, seem harmless?

The truth is that a migrating colony of millions of army ants is deadly dangerous to any creature that fails to run away. From elephants to beetles, army ants will attack and devour whatever they can catch. To many minds, the ultimate predator is not a shark or lion, they can be stopped. But a migrating army ant colony is unstoppable. Kill a thousand army ants, kill a *million* army ants, and 10 million will be right behind to take their place in the attack.

"Death by Numbers"

The queen had died. It only happened once in a century that a queen died without producing a brood of fertile daughters to take her place. The queen of an army ant colony produces every ant in the colony. Without a queen, the colony cannot survive.

Suddenly the 20 million ants in this vast colony had no queen. The news passed like lightning from antennae to antennae, from worker to worker. The ants convey no fear, grief, panic, but rather just the practical instructions that scouts needed to find a new queen or a new colony this one could join.

In two days, contact was made with a colony in the middle of its migration to a new home nest sight. The two colonies merged.

Now an unstoppable sea of 60 million ants, covering a quarter of a square mile in a dense, moving carpet of hungry, meat-eating carnivores, was on the move through the Peruvian forests of South America. The size of eight football fields, or 1,000 school buses, this mass of ants was after food and a new site for a home nest. Sixty million is such a large number that, if one ant passed a marker every second, it would take over two years for these ants to pass the marker.

When smaller foraging parties of only 50,000 to 100,000 ants roamed the forest, leading worker ants built side walls of dirt to protect the marchers. They would march in a thick stream several inches wide and many yards long.

But this was no foraging party. This was a great migration by an oversized colony with an enormous number of ants. No walls or barricades were built as the colony streamed forward.

There was no chaos in this mass movement. On the contrary, the colony moved with military precision. Order was created by chemical scents. Lead scouts (soldier ants and large workers) laid down a trail scent for every other ant to follow. The queen created a colony scent that drew every ant to stay packed into the living, black carpet.

The ants in the army were not all the same. The biggest were soldier ants. Soldiers were paler, almost blond in color, with fierce biting mandibles (mouth parts similar to fangs and jaws) that were long, curved, and pointed like a steer's horns. They were also armed with

From *Close Encounters with Deadly Dangers*. © 1998 Kendall Haven. Libraries Unlimited. (800) 237-6124.

working multi-faceted, or compound, eyes and with mildly poison-ous stingers. Soldiers marched at the edges as guards and protectors.

There were three sizes of worker ants, all sterile females, and all dark red to black. Workers had shorter cutting mandibles, not as good for biting and attack, but much better at cutting up and dissecting. Workers had only poor, single-lens eyes. The smallest size of workers handled eggs and larvae as brood nurses. The two bigger sizes simply marched now, but did the real work of hunting, hauling, and building for the colony.

Somewhere in the middle of the ant sea walked the queen. She was shiny black, over three times the size of the biggest soldier, and blind. She looked more like a termite queen than an ant. The final section of her body, the gaster, was bloated and distended. This one part of the queen produced three million eggs each month.

Workers lived almost a year. Soldiers lived for one to one and one-half years; the queen for up to five.

A few males traveled with this massive colony. They had wings and looked more like wasps. Their only job was to fertilize the queen's eggs; and they contributed nothing else to the colony.

The army traveled at a leisurely pace of about 60 feet per hour, not because the ants couldn't walk faster, but because the lead ants almost had to be forced to advance into new territory. They, like all army ants, would have been much happier to have chemical odors (trail scents) to follow.

Every living creature either fled in terror before this great army or died. However, a few special species of birds and butterflies purpose-fully traveled with them, hovering above the leading edge of the army. The birds wanted the sweat grubs and beetles the army flushed out of hiding as it advanced.

At night the army stopped. Rather than dig temporary tunnels and nests, the worker ants formed hanging baskets out of their own bodies, attached to tree trunks or low limbs. Almost half a million ants clung together to create each hanging bivouac nest. The queen and the millions of larvae the colony carried with it were safely tucked into the middle of these hanging nests.

The nests formed with amazing speed and with no hint of confusion or uncertainty. As one worker started a nest, she gave off a chemical scent, a recruiting signal, that told others to follow her. Each new recruit added to the strength of this chemical signal. Once the

From *Close Encounters with Deadly Dangers*. © 1998 Kendall Haven. Libraries Unlimited. (800) 237-6124.

nest was full and could hold no more without danger of falling, a different odor was sent through the ants to make newcomers turn away.

The conversion from a one-quarter-square-mile living carpet of ants to hanging bivouac nests took less than half an hour.

Army ants live in a world controlled by smells. Smells direct where they go and what they do. Smells identify their home, their paths, and dangers. Scents are the magic communications system that make 60 million act as one.

In the morning it was time to forage and gather food before continuing the march to a new home site. All army ant colonies periodically migrate to a new home nest site. Some species make these moves like clockwork once every 35 days, while some wait until the food supply around their current home has been depleted before they move. The migrations usually last for several weeks before a new home site is reached.

Soldier ants and the biggest worker ants were the first to descend from the bivouac nests. They would be the leading fighters and attackers on the raid. Medium-sized workers followed. They were porters and would carry food back to the nests.

At first the ants seemed to fan out randomly. Soon a chemical signal was relayed that a small group of local ants had been found. Seemingly as one, the army ants turned in that direction and followed the trail scents toward this food supply. While army ants will eat whatever they catch, their primary diet is non-army ants and small lizards, beetles, and scorpions. Army ants couldn't individually overpower any of these, but when they work collectively, each is an easy target.

A solid, six-inch-wide stream of ants now poured into the raid, looking like the trunk of a great tree. At its head, the ants fanned into a solid swarm, now 200 feet wide and many feet thick. The leading edge of this swarm probed under and behind every rock, pebble, and leaf for some hiding treat.

A lizard mistakenly popped its head out of a hole. It tried to retreat, but was instantly swarmed. It tried to eat the ants, but for every one it ate, fifty raced onto its head and body, biting, tearing, stinging. And then the worker ants swarmed in, cutting the lizard into countless thousands of tiny pieces, each of which were hauled by single workers back to the nests. Some larger pieces were cooperatively hauled and dragged by a group of workers.

From *Close Encounters with Deadly Dangers.* © 1998 Kendall Haven. Libraries Unlimited. (800) 237-6124.

As a massive cluster of thousands of ants crowded around the lizard, the swarm front moved on. A thick stream of many thousands of new ants poured into the swarm every minute.

Near the base of a tree, they found a scorpion hiding behind a rock. The scorpion clicked its claws and lashed with its poisonous tail in vain. If it killed five, a hundred, or a thousand ants, it wouldn't matter. There were a thousand times a thousand waiting behind to take their place. There was literally no way to defeat army ants. The scorpion had to run or die.

Beetles, centipedes, and worms were caught and devoured. A tree squirrel slipped and fell from the safety of overhead branches. Before it could rise to its feet it was covered black with ants. Unable to see, it ran in circles for a few moments before collapsing. In less than two minutes every part of the squirrel was cut up for ant food. Only the bones were left.

Soon the line of workers hauling the spoils of war back to the nests grew thicker than the line of new workers pouring out to the swarm front. Each worker carried her load slung underneath her body. The best haulers were those with the longest legs.

By noon the swarm front halted. At a signal sent from the nests, every ant turned and streamed back down the trunk line. The raid was over. It was time to continue the migration march.

By 1:00 P.M., the great army was again on the move, shockingly big, dense, and lethal. Guides led the great mass through the open forest floor and along the edge of a wide meadow. They drove all living things in front of them as surely as a forest fire does.

Along one flank, an alarm sounded. Several soldier ants reared onto their hind legs, released alarm chemical scent, vibrated their antennae, and opened and closed their fierce mandibles—the signs of a general alarm. In response, a wedge of open space began to form near the soldiers issuing the alarm, like Moses parting the Red Sea.

A wild boar, 120 pounds of fighting muscle and sharp tusks, thundered across the meadow toward the migrating army. Mammals can easily outrun an ant army, but stand no chance of surviving if they are caught. Without pausing to assess the danger, the boar stumbled into the army while fleeing a panther.

In a sudden panicked realization of its new predicament, the boar trampled thousands of ants with its hooves. But tens of thousands more streamed up each leg, biting and stinging as they climbed.

From *Close Encounters with Deadly Dangers.* © 1998 Kendall Haven. Libraries Unlimited. (800) 237-6124.

The first soldier ants to climb and attack the boar knew to aim for its eyes. Blinded, the boar stumbled in tormented agony as a living black curtain of ants covered its body.

The boar was no longer visible. It was now just a three-foot-tall blob of endless black ants. In only a minute the pig stumbled and collapsed to the ground. It was completely devoured in five minutes. All that was left were white bones.

The army marched on as if the boar had never existed.

In another week they would reach a new home nest sight and the worker ants would toil non-stop until the complex of new tunnels, chambers, and nests had been dug. Then the colony would split. Sixty million was too many for one colony to support.

The queen would produce a brood of fertile daughters. The worker ants would pick the queens they would follow. The rest of the daughters would be eaten. Life would continue for the army ants as it has for countless thousands of years.

Thinking About This Ecosystem

Rain forests are known for their great diversity of species. Do you think army ants help maintain diversity, or diminish it? (*Actually, they help maintain it. Army ants feed in one area and then move on, not returning to that same area for several years. Within the area a colony visits, some areas have been newly cleared of most ants, beetles, and other insects; other areas are just rebuilding their insect population bases; and other areas have a thriving, well-established insect population. Like forest fires that periodically clear away old growth to make way for new, the periodic feeding of army ants helps promote new growth of diverse insect populations.*)

Are there elements of the ecosystem that benefit from the presence of army ants? (*Like all ants, army ants aerate the ground with their extensive networks of tunnels. They also help control insect overpopulation.*) What else can you find that they do?

Several species of birds and butterflies travel with the army ants. Do the ants gain anything from this relationship? (*No, but they are not harmed by it either.*)

See if you can make lists of the species (1) that are benefited by the activity of army ants, (2) that are mostly unaffected by army ants, and (3) that are severely affected by army ants. Are there species that prey on army ants? (*No. Even those species that eat ants find it is much safer to stay away from army ants.*)

From *Close Encounters with Deadly Dangers*. © 1998 Kendall Haven. Libraries Unlimited. (800) 237-6124.

Thinking About This Predator

Army ant colonies are "caught in an interesting bind." On the one hand, the more ants the better. More ants makes the colony safer and better able to ensure its survival. On the other hand, more ants means more mouths to feed. It means the colony uses up the food resources in one area faster and has to move more often.

Ant colonies tend to grow until they can no longer support themselves. Then, like a uranium atom in a nuclear reactor, the colony splits into two smaller groups. The queen seems to know that the colony is too big to survive, and produces a brood of fertile females and males. The workers seem to know, and look for a new group of queens to evaluate. Each worker picks the queen it will follow. Those queens who do not win the support of a colony-sized group are eaten. Each surviving queen picks several males, and the new colonies march off to their own development, each ant knowing exactly what its role will be in this new colony.

Army ants succeed because they act as a coordinated group. Group hunting allows ants to attack, and live on, species that a lone army ant would have no chance of overcoming. In effect, group hunting changes the ants' position, or niche, in the ecosystem. It allows them to act like top predators, instead of being in the lowly position held by other ants who act more as individuals.

Here are some questions you can research about army ants in the library and on the Internet:

1. What are the advantages and disadvantages of size? Army ants act like one giant predator. Acting like a single big predator, instead of 20 million small ones, makes it easier for the colony to survive. But is bigger always better? Would a colony of 100,000 ants survive better than a colony of 1,000,000? Why? Would a colony of 100,000,000 ants survive better? What are the disadvantages of size? What is the biggest predator you can find? What is the smallest? Does a predator have to be an animal? Can a germ be a predator? Can a virus?

2. Army ants survive because they have developed fast and accurate ways to communicate with each other. They can all send chemical signals, and they all follow the signals they receive. Make a list of all the different signals army ants send to each other and how those signals are sent.

Additional Reading

Here are references for information about army ants and the tropical jungle ecosystem. See your librarian for additional titles available at your local library.

Beckers, R., and S. Goss. "Colony Size, Communication and Ant Foraging Strategies." *Psyche* 96 (1989): 239–56.

Billen, J. "Origin of the Trail Pheromone in Echitoninae." In *Biology and Evolution of Social Insects*, edited by J. Billen. Leuven, Belgium: Leuven University Press, 1992.

Breed, M., and C. Michener, eds. *The Biology of Social Insects: Proceedings of the Ninth Congress of the International Union for the Study of Social Insects.* Boulder, CO: Westview Press, 1982.

Brenner, Barbara. *If You Were an Ant. . . .* New York: Harper & Row, 1973.

Burton, J., and N. Franks. "The Foraging Ecology of the Army Ant." *Ecological Entomology* 10 (1985): 131–41.

Chadab, R., and C. Rettenmyer. "Mass Recruitment by Army Ants." *Science* 188 (1975): 1124–25.

Costello, David. *The World of the Ant.* Philadelphia: Lippincott, 1968.

Demuth, Patricia. *Those Amazing Ants.* New York: MacMillan, 1994.

Fischer-Nagel, Heiderose. *An Ant Colony.* Minneapolis, MN: Carolrhoda Books, 1994.

Franks, N. "Army Ants: A Collective Intelligence." *American Scientist* 77 (2) (1989): 138–45.

Franks, N., and C. Fletcher. "Spatial Patterns in Army Ant Foraging and Migration." *Behavioral Ecology* 12 (1983): 261–70.

Golley, F., ed. *Tropical Rain Forest Ecosystems: Structure and Function.* Elsevier, Amsterdam: Ecosystems of the World, 1983.

Gotward, William. *Army Ants.* Ithaca, NY: Cornell University Press, 1995.

Hogue, Charles. *The Armies of the Ants.* New York: World Publications, 1972.

Holldobler, Bert. *Journey to the Ants.* Cambridge, MA: Belknap Press, 1994.

Hoyt, Erich. *The Earth Dwellers.* New York: Simon & Schuster, 1996.

Ordish, George. *The Year of the Ant.* New York: Charles Scribner's Sons, 1978.

Overbeck, Cynthia. *Ants.* Minneapolis, MN: Lerner Publication, 1982.

Pasteels, M., ed. *From Individual to Collective Behavior in Social Insects.* Basel, Switzerland: Les Treilles Workshop Proceedings, 1987.

Pitt, Valerie. *A Closer Look at Ants*. New York: Franklin Watts, 1975.

Schneirla, T. "The Army Ant." *Scientific America* 178 (6) (1968): 16–23.

Selsam, Millicent. *Questions and Answers About Ants*. New York: Four Winds Press, 1977.

Stephenson, Carl. "Leiningen Versus the Ants." In *Great Tales of Action and Adventure*, edited by George Bennet. New York: Dell, 1959.

Terry, Trevor. *The Life Cycle of an Ant*. New York: Bookwright, 1988.

Topoff, H., and J. Mirenda. "Army Ants on the Move: Relationship Between Food Supply and Emigration Frequency." *Science* 207 (1980): 1099–1100.

———. "Army Ants Do Not Eat and Run." *Animal Behavior* 28 (1980): 1040–45.

Topoff, H., J. Mirenda, and R. Droual. "Behavioral Ecology of Mass Recruitment in Army Ants." *Animal Behavior* 28 (1980): 779–89.

Deadly Desert Dancer

Scorpions of the Southwest American Desert

At a Glance

Scorpions are an ancient species. Evidence suggests that they were the first arachnid to crawl onto the earth. Scorpions have spread to cover every corner of the tropical and semi-tropical world. They live in, and have adapted to, swamps, forests, jungles, and arid deserts.

Like an unwanted stray dog, scorpions prefer to live close to humans, liking the nooks and crannies of human habitats and the other insects who are drawn to humans, especially flies, spiders, and cockroaches.

Scorpions look dangerous. They look mean, eight scuttling legs, two lobster-like pincers on long front arms, a hardened, shell-like body, and a poisonous tail arched high overhead.

Humans suffer almost 150,000 poisonous scorpion bites each year, including over 1,200 fatalities, more than can be attributed to all poisonous snakes combined.

Maybe because of their deadly interactions with humans, scorpions have held important positions in the mythology of Mexico and parts of the Old World for their toughness, persistence, and survival instinct. Scorpions are a fascinating case study in successful adaptive biology. But don't study *too* closely: the sting of a scorpion is truly a deadly danger.

"Deadly Desert Dancer"

Shimmering heat waves rose from sand and rock as if they were giant griddles. Even the sparse tumbleweeds and sage seemed to suffer from the terrible heat. A lone horse and rider plodded slowly across this rough southern Arizona landscape. It had been a long ride. As they paused at the edge of this low butte, the cluster of buildings and corrals that was their ranch spread out below them. They were home.

The rider lifted his wide-brimmed hat and wiped his brow with a sleeve. He adjusted his hat back low over his eyes to block out the blinding glare and, with a quick flick of the reins, started his horse down the gradual, rocky slope.

Nearing the bottom, two of the horse's feet began to slide on loose pebbles and shale. The horse pranced high to regain its balance, kicking up sprays of dust and dirt. One foot flipped aside a large rock at the trail's edge.

The horse bucked and kicked, its eyes growing wide and white with fear. A six-inch-long scorpion had been resting under the rock and now scurried forward as if to attack. It made fierce warning clicks and snapped its front pincers. Its slender, segmented tail arched high over its body, poison sack and needle-sharp stinger waving their threats at the intruders.

"Steady girl," called the rider. He patted the horse's flank as he clutched the saddle horn with his other hand to keep from being thrown off.

The horse quieted and nervously edged away from the scorpion.

"It's just a scorpion, girl. It won't attack."

But, in truth, it would. A scorpion knows no fear. It lives a very primitive, basic life: Hide from the heat of the sun; eat when food presents itself; and kill everything that threatens, resists, or gets in the way.

From *Close Encounters with Deadly Dangers*. © 1998 Kendall Haven. Libraries Unlimited. (800) 237-6124.

The scorpion continued to dance from side to side, three quick steps one way, two quick steps back, inching forward, snapping its claws in threat and warning, waving its deadly tail.

Rider and horse turned back toward the barn and home. The scorpion was left alone to seek shelter from the burning heat of the sun.

The pink-and-sand colored scorpion turned down the same trail, seeking a cool, dark spot to rest for the day.

Scorpions are the most ancient member of the arachnid family. They were most certainly the first arachnid (eight-legged creature) to crawl on land. There are over 650 species of scorpions spread throughout the tropical and sub-tropical regions of the world. Some have adapted to damp, swampy places, some to forest, and some to desert.

The desert species include the deadliest of all scorpions, though not the largest. The lobster scorpions of Sumatra measure over a foot long. American desert scorpions rarely exceed six inches.

With eight legs (four on each side); powerful front pincers; a hard, shell-like casing over the body; and a curving, poisonous tail ending in a single, thorn-like stinger, scorpions are the invincible tanks of the desert. They are also the perfect survivors. They can live without food for half a year, and can survive being submerged under water for a day and frozen for several weeks.

Nocturnal by nature, scorpions also avoid the sun to keep from depleting their precious body fluids. They need a steady supply of water, but get most of it from the food they eat. A desert scorpion can comfortably survive on a diet of one cockroach per week, but will eat more if it is available.

Marching downhill toward the ranch, the scorpion passed through the shade of a large rock. Drawn by the dark and cool, the scorpion crawled around its base, searching for a way to get underneath. Braced at an angle against another rock, this rock actually formed a wide ledge over a shallow pit, the perfect spot for a scorpion to rest through the daylight hours.

The only problem was that there was already a scorpion under this rock. It is said that if two scorpions are under the same rock, they are either mating or one is eating the other. Scorpions are not territorial. They simply hate other scorpions and will usually fight to the death upon meeting.

From *Close Encounters with Deadly Dangers*. © 1998 Kendall Haven. Libraries Unlimited. (800) 237-6124.

The invading scorpion sprang forward. The defender, having been alerted by its sensors that another scorpion was near, turned to meet the attack. Pincers locked with pincers. Muscles strained, trying to twist the enemy off balance and gain an advantage. A tug-of-war ensued that looked more like a dance as the two enemies pushed and shoved each other around the pit.

Each tried to flip its opponent on its back, where it could easily be killed. Each tried to free a pincer to strike at leg joints and cripple the other. Each tried to rise high enough to let the tip of its poisonous tail lash forward and do its deadly work. Each tried to avoid the other's tail. Liquid poison glistened on the tip of each stinger.

The invader freed one pincer and locked onto the base of the defender's pincer, sawing through the joint. The defender flipped and twisted, slashing its tail through the air in an attempt to escape the hold.

But the invader was strong and careful. In a moment the pincer had been severed and lay useless in the dirt. The invader now had a major advantage. The defender scurried away, giving up the shelter of the pit to the newcomer.

The invading scorpion settled into the cool of its new home-for-a-day to wait for dark. Two battles had made the scorpion hungry. Tonight it would hunt in earnest down closer to the human's buildings.

Scorpions have learned to prefer living around humans. It isn't that they like humans; they don't. Humans, along with other scorpions, an occasional hawk, and drought, are a scorpion's only enemies. But two things come with humans that scorpions need. First, humans build and make lots of dark, cool nooks and crannies (drawers, boots, mattresses, wood stacks, barns, etc.), which are perfect places to hide from the sun's heat. Second, many of a scorpion's favorite foods (flies, cockroaches, small mice, and ants) thrive around humans.

As the last reds of sunset faded from a star-filled sky, the scorpion began its hunt. It would have preferred that some meal stumble into its lair, but, since none had appeared through the long afternoon, it would now go in search of dinner.

A scorpion's eyes are crude and almost useless. Scorpions sense the world around them by feeling vibrations. Short hairs along their front legs and pincers are really tiny receiving antennae pointing in every direction. They detect any vibration in the air that would mean movement nearby.

From *Close Encounters with Deadly Dangers*. © 1998 Kendall Haven. Libraries Unlimited. (800) 237-6124.

A pair of long, comb-like sensor organs, called *pectines*, drape from a scorpion's abdomen to touch the ground and sense vibrations traveling through the earth. A scorpion has no ears to hear and no nose to smell, but through the size and pattern of these air and ground vibrations it builds a composite picture of the world around it.

As the scorpion passed under a wooden fence and into the shadow of a large trough, it sensed nearby movement in a familiar pattern. A cockroach! No, more than one—several cockroaches nearby.

The scorpion's claws, which are normally tucked back against its chest, extended and opened. The deadly tail, which normally lies flat behind, curved up over its body, ready to strike if it met any resistance.

Now the scorpion had to be careful. Cockroaches were fast. If alarmed, they would scatter. The scorpion had to anticipate their movement and position itself where the roaches would come to it. Slowly it crept sideways, always facing toward the vibrations.

It stopped, waiting. One set of vibrations grew stronger. A cockroach scampered in this direction.

The vibrations grew stronger . . . now!

The scorpion lunged forward. One claw locked onto the thick body of a well-fed cockroach and dragged it back. The scorpion pounced on its victim, seizing it with its claws and legs, and literally tore the roach apart. A scorpion's poison is rarely used during a hunt unless the intended prey puts up a strong fight.

Scorpions' mouths are very small. They must tear their food into tiny bits before they eat. The scorpion would need time to devour the soft tissues and precious moisture from this roach's body.

But the scorpion was interrupted by new vibrations, massive vibrations. It was the animal humans call a dog. The scorpion could feel the rumbling vibrations made by its great paws and the pulsing vibrations in the air of its constant sniffing as it searched the far end of the trough.

Hovering over its catch, the scorpion assumed combat position, claws out, tail raised.

The vibrations grew sharper and nearer. The dog was searching, sniffing, following a scent. The scorpion slowly turned to face straight toward the growing vibrations.

From *Close Encounters with Deadly Dangers.* © 1998 Kendall Haven. Libraries Unlimited. (800) 237-6124.

The scorpion could feel the hot breath of the dog as it curiously studied the insect. The dog, almost a hundred times bigger than this scorpion, leaned closer to sniff.

The scorpion's tail lashed forward, a tiny drop of poison gleaming at its tip.

The dog howled in pain and surprise and bounded back. The hole that stinger made in the dog's nose was very small, but the scorpion's poison was a powerful toxin, similar to, but more concentrated, than many snakes' venom.

As the dog yelped with the burning pain that spread up its face, and as humans ran into the corral to see what had happened, the scorpion finished its meal and scurried off.

Within an hour the dog had died. The scorpion felt no remorse, no sense of sorrow. It had no real thought at all. It was just a desert war machine struggling to survive and to destroy whatever got in its way.

Thinking About This Ecosystem

What is a desert? (*A desert is defined as a large area where there isn't enough vegetation to support human life.*) A desert ecosystem is a harsh environment in which everything seems to struggle to survive, including plants. Can you name the major limiting factors to life in the desert? (*Many think heat is a limiting factor for the desert, but tropical jungles are also hot. The key limiting factor is water. Water limits grass and plant life, which controls the number of herbivores [grazers and browsers] the system can support, which, in turn, controls the number of carnivores, or predators. Add water and the desert would turn into a lush garden and attract a much greater variety of animal life.*)

Which plants survive best in the desert? Can you determine how and why they survive better than other plants? (*If water is the key limiting factor, look at the way these plants absorb and hold water as a key to their ability to survive in the desert.*)

Which animals survive best in the desert? Make a list of successful desert animals. Do they have common characteristics that make it easier for them to survive? (*Animals have two big problems in the desert: Lack of water and the scarcity of food. Those that survive best have learned how to adapt to both problems.*)

Where are there deserts in the world? Mark all the deserts you can find on a map. How many are hot? Are there some far north and far south that are very cold instead of very hot? Is the Arctic a desert? Is the Antarctic? (*Yes to both questions.*)

From *Close Encounters with Deadly Dangers*. © 1998 Kendall Haven. Libraries Unlimited. (800) 237-6124.

Thinking About This Predator

Scorpions can be found in tropical and sub-tropical environments all over the world. Some live in deserts, some in swamps, and some in cool forests. Some scorpion species are not poisonous at all, and some have only mild, locally numbing poison. Some, like the one in this story, carry deadly neurotoxin. Why do you think scorpions show such variety and can be found in so many different types of ecosystems? (*Scorpions are an excellent example of adaptive evolution. Over countless centuries, they have adapted to, and specialized for, their local environment. The inability of a species to change and adapt is the most common reason for a species becoming extinct. Those that can adapt to the widest range of environmental conditions have the best chance for species survival.*)

Unique in the insect world, scorpions have actual intercourse as mammals do and give live births. Scorpions never scatter far from the sight of their birth. Thus scorpions are slow to migrate and take over new territories as environments change. Instead, over time, scorpions change to match their environment.

Here are some questions you can research about scorpions in the library and on the Internet:

1. Why would scorpions want to live in the harsh desert? What advantages do they gain from living there?

2. The most poisonous scorpion species all live in deserts. This is generally also true for snakes. Desert snakes tend to be more poisonous than non-desert snakes. Why? What features of life in the desert would make stronger poison a necessity?

Additional Reading

Here are references for information about scorpions and the desert ecosystem. See your librarian for additional titles available at your local library.

Alexander, A. "On the Stridulation of Scorpions." *Behavior* 12 (1968): 339–52.

Bettini, S., ed. *Arthropod Venoms.* New York: Springer-Verlag, 1978.

Billings, Charlene. *Scorpions.* New York: Dodd, Mead, 1983.

Cloudsley-Thompson, J. *Spiders, Scorpions, Centipedes and Mites.* New York: Pergamon Press, 1968.

———. *Spiders and Scorpions.* New York: McGraw-Hill, 1974.

Cooper, Jason. *Scorpions.* New York: Rowke Book, 1996.

De Vosjoli, Philippe. *Arachnomania.* Lakeside, CA: Advanced Vivarium Systems, 1991.

Green, Tamara. *Scorpions (Creepy Crawly Collection)*. Minneapolis, MN: Gareth Stevens, 1996.

Habermehl, Gerhard. *Venomous Animals and Their Toxins*. New York: Springer-Verlag, 1981.

Myers, Walter. *Scorpions*. New York: HarperCollins, 1988.

Polis, Gary. *The Biology of Scorpions*. Palo Alto, CA: Stanford University Press, 1990.

Pringle, Lawrence, and Gary Polis. *Scorpion Man—Exploring the World of Scorpions*. New York: Atheneum, 1994.

Storad, Conrad. *Scorpions*. Minneapolis, MN: Lerner Publications, 1995.

Ꞧawk Ꞓyes

Red-Tailed Hawks of the American Midwest

At a Glance

A hawk is a raptor, one of the noble descendants of the fierce hunting dinosaurs, including the well-known velociraptor. Raptor birds (hawks, falcons, eagles, owls, and osprey) have always been viewed as majestic, powerful, and regal. Falconry, the taming and training of these birds, is known as the sport of kings. An eagle is our national symbol. Owls in the Middle East have been thought to be both magic and harbingers of powerful evil.

Raptors are predator birds, essential elements in the ecosystems that support them. They are swift, intelligent, fierce, and cunning. Hawks, especially, soar through the skies and through our dreams as images of powerful freedom: freedom from care, from fear, even freedom from gravity itself, which binds us to the ground.

In reality, a hawk's life is far from carefree. Like street urchins, hawks must train themselves from birth to be ruthless survivors, or they will perish. They may be beautiful to watch as they soar through the heavens, but their minds are not on beauty or leisure as the fly. They are in a constant battle for food and survival.

"Ḣawk Eyes"

The first snows of November silently swirled over the field. A female red-tailed hawk shifted in her perch on a top limb of a towering beech tree and again shook off the flakes as they piled on her shoulders. Her oily feathers easily shed rain, but snow didn't slide off without a good shake.

An hour ago everything she could see—bare woods, empty fields, and small meadow—was colored in bleak shades of dull brown. Now a luster of glowing white sparkled over her domain.

Hawks are watchers. This hawk watched intently as the first snow of her life fell around her. From her perch she could see for miles across the flat fields and low rolling hills of southern Illinois.

Movement between two of the long field rows caught her eye: a mouse, 200 yards away. The snow was forgotten. The hawk focused her great eyes on this lone gray field mouse struggling through the snow in search of food.

Hawks, like the other raptors (eagles, falcons, osprey, and owls—all direct descendants of the fiercest of the dinosaur predators), have the best eyesight in the world. Though her head was a tiny fraction of the size of a human head, her eyes were almost as big as a human child's.

Hawk eyes are telescopic. That is, they can be adjusted like a telescopic zoom lens on a camera to focus on objects far away.

More important, the retina of a hawk's eye is packed with many times more light-sensitive cones than a human's, to record far more detail. These extra cones allow a hawk to distinguish an object from its background five or six times farther away than a human could. The hawk can see a spider web at 80 yards and a beetle at 150. To use their great eyesight, hawks hunt during the day. Their cousins, the owls, rule the night.

The hawk spread her great wings, flapped hard twice, and lifted into the air. Like all hawks, her body was wide, thick, even chunky for a bird. Her wings spread to over five feet and were not only longer but also broader than most birds' wings.

Rather than swooping straight for the field mouse, the hawk flew into a nearby thermal current and spiraled higher, gliding with the

From *Close Encounters with Deadly Dangers*. © 1998 Kendall Haven. Libraries Unlimited. (800) 237-6124.

upward air currents. While not the fastest flyers, hawks are among the world's best soarers and have an uncanny ability to find and ride every thermal (upward spiraling current of slightly warmer air). Glider pilots need to catch thermals to stay aloft and have learned to follow hawks to find them.

The hawk sailed out of the thermal 1,400 feet above the field, wings held straight out, soaring slowly through the falling flakes, eyes locked on every move and twitch of the mouse over one-quarter mile below, still watching, observing, as she soared high above.

She dipped the feathers of her left wing tip and raised the red feathers of her long, fan-shaped tail. The slight shift plunged her into a power dive towards earth. She retracted her wings halfway to provide stability and less drag. She didn't flap during her dive. She had become a screeching, gravity-powered rocket. Her hard beak split the air as she hurtled toward the field at 140 miles per hour. Snow streaked past her in blurs as she rocketed toward her prey.

Hawks can't attack as fast as falcons, who screech in at over 200 miles per hour. But at 140 miles per hour, this hawk would cover the final 200 feet of her attack (the length of four and one-half school buses) in one second.

From the pine trees at the edge of the field a squirrel spotted the attacking hawk and chattered its noisy alarm. The mouse spun and scampered for the safety of its hole. The hawk shifted its wings and adjusted its angle of descent to intercept the fleeing meal just before it disappeared to safety.

Her thick yellow legs, which had been pressed back against her body, swung forward like the landing gear of a jet. Her long claws, her talons, eagerly tore at the snow-filled air, waiting to seize her prey.

The squirrel continued to chatter its alarm. The mouse sped for its hole, leaving a thick trail through the building snow.

With less than a second to go, the hawk arched her wings to lift the upper part of her body, slow her descent, and ram her deadly claws forward into the attack.

As the mouse dove for safety, the hawk's great claws snapped shut, nipping only a small piece of mouse tail. It had escaped. She soared back into the sky, screeching her anger and frustration: *keeeeea! keeeeea!* The piercing sound echoed across the still field, causing all small animals to shudder.

From *Close Encounters with Deadly Dangers.* © 1998 Kendall Haven. Libraries Unlimited. (800) 237-6124.

In less than 20 seconds the hawk was back on her perch atop the beech tree, watching, observing, hunting with her magnificent eyes.

It had always been like this for the hawk, for every hawk. They live on the edge, staying alive by their cunning and their persistence. Hawks that don't perfect their hunting skills, starve.

The hawk had been hatched in mid-April, high in a sugar pine tree less than 50 yards from where she now sat. Hawks build big nests. She and her two brothers shared one four feet across and three feet high.

She learned early that life would only come to those who took. Her parents fed the one who pushed hardest to the front and squawked the loudest. One brother slept more, shoved less, and seemed always to politely step aside. He rarely got fed and stayed small.

On his first flight (three days after the other two had learned to use their wings), that brother was swept over a ridge into another meadow by a strong wind. No one went to look for him or to assist. Each hawk had to teach itself to fly and to hunt. This was part of being a hawk.

The female hawk spent the summer learning to control and master her flights with her one surviving brother. They would get no help from their parents or other hawks. Together they spiraled high into the sky, dancing through loop rolls and S spins. Together they swirled through practice dives and learned about successful hunting. Together they learned to use their sharp, hooked beaks to tear through their victims.

Together they learned both the magic power of their great claws, and the danger. Hawk claws seem oversized for their bodies: Three curved, razor-sharp toe claws in front, one heel claw in back. Hawk claws actually lock when they seize a prey. That is their secret. Like a trap snapping shut, hawk talons lock onto an animal and will not, *cannot* let go.

Even the hawk, itself, can't release its grip without pushing hard against some solid surface. Normally a hawk swoops down, snatches a helpless rodent, carries it away to a safe perch, and then shoves the now-dead victim's body hard against a tree branch or rock. Like a spring-loaded trigger, that push releases the talons' grip. Nothing escapes from the grip of a hawk.

From *Close Encounters with Deadly Dangers.* © 1998 Kendall Haven. Libraries Unlimited. (800) 237-6124.

In mid-summer the female hawk's brother learned the danger of that system. A hawk's hearing is almost as superior as its eyesight. From his perch, her brother heard a rustling in the meadow and soared into the air to investigate.

Slithering over a bare spot, a thick snake emerged from the tall summer grass. Her brother plunged into his diving attack. His talons extended and locked onto the snake, cutting deeply into its back. The snake writhed and coiled, flipping the hawk onto his side.

Only then did her brother realize that this snake was over six feet long and much too heavy for him to lift. The young hawk and the snake tumbled across the grass, twisting and flailing. Flipped onto his back, the hawk couldn't make his talons release because there was nothing but snake and air to push against. He was locked in a fight he could not win.

The snake looped a thick coil of its body over the hawk, trapping his wings. They rolled through the meadow, locked together, the snake hissing and biting, the hawk screeching and pecking, becoming entwined in the long grass and tall weeds.

Completely tied in twisted ropes of grass and snake, the hawk couldn't move. He and the snake lay there in the meadow until a weasel found them both.

The female hawk alone, had survived that first dangerous summer. Red-tailed hawks can live 20 to 23 years, but over half die in their first summer.

In the fall many hawks migrated south. The female hawk did not feel the urge to go. She felt rooted in her meadow and fields. She decided to stay. A few others stayed in these fields and woods with her. It was better this way. Less food would be available in the winter.

Watching from her perch, the hawk spotted a pair of rabbits edging along the tree line. A rabbit makes a bountiful feast for a hawk. Mostly she lived on smaller rodents (mice, shrews, moles, and ground squirrels) and on small blackbirds, quail, and pheasants. Rabbits, though, are a favorite target of hawks.

The female hawk flapped her wings, spread her tail fan, and lifted from her perch. Finding a thermal, she soared to 1,500 feet above the field. She controlled her flight with the long feathers at the ends, or tips, of her wings. Power came from the mid-sections of her thick wings.

From *Close Encounters with Deadly Dangers.* © 1998 Kendall Haven. Libraries Unlimited. (800) 237-6124.

She soared and watched, wings spread, gliding high above the field where she would not be noticed. One of the rabbits hopped into the open and started on a diagonal path across one corner of the field.

The hawk plunged into a power dive, wings shortened and held tight, body streamlined. Like a streaking arrow she shot downward.

A squirrel in the trees chattered its warning. The rabbit paused, lifted its head, and twitched its nose to assess the danger. It spotted the hawk's shadow, growing rapidly from a tiny speck.

Frantically, it bounded for the safety of the woods. But it had hesitated too long. Like a screeching thunderbolt, the hawk slammed into her prey at over 100 miles per hour. Both tumbled across the snow-filled rows of the barren field.

As if smashed by a speeding car, the rabbit died instantly, crushed by the impact. The hawk rose and shook her feathers. She hopped onto her prize and locked her talons deep into its flesh. With great, slow flappings of her wings that "whooshed" loudly across the field, she rose into the air and carried her dinner to her lofty perch.

Securing the rabbit's body in a crook of the tree she cried her triumph: *keeeeea!, keeeeea!* The piercing sound traveled for miles across the desolate countryside. This rabbit would satisfy her for days.

As the snow storm ended, she finished her meal, and resumed her watchful perch high in the beech tree.

Thinking About This Ecosystem

What are the major groups of living things in a North American woods and meadow ecosystem? (*First, primary ground plant production: grasses, weeds, bushes, flowers, moss, and fungus. Second, trees. Third, plant eaters: small rodents, mammals, and insects. Fourth, small carnivores: lizards, insects, small birds, and small mammals. Fifth, top predators: weasels, foxes, snakes, raptors, etc. And, finally, scavengers and decomposers, which recycle the leftover scraps back into dirt.*)

Which of these general populations is most important to the ecosystem's survival? (*Plants. Without plants, no other group survives, but grasses could survive without any of the other groups. Trees need decomposers to clear away the remains of dead trees.*)

What would happen if the top predators were eliminated from this ecosystem? (*Initially there would be a population explosion of the meadow species the top predators eat, such as rabbits and mice. Next, these excessive plant-eater*

From *Close Encounters with Deadly Dangers.* © 1998 Kendall Haven. Libraries Unlimited. (800) 237-6124.

populations would overgraze the area and kill the grass crop. Finally, there would be a major die-off of mice and rabbits as grasses became scarce. The result would be a much weaker, less diverse, less healthy, and less productive ecosystem.) This exact scenario has happened in a number of areas in the United States where all large predators and game species were killed, either for sport or to protect domestic animals. Do you think it is good, even necessary, to have predators in a natural ecosystem?

How do you think meadow species survive the winter when grass stops growing and is buried under snow? See if you can find the answer in the library or on the Internet.

Thinking About This Predator

There are 200 species of hawks worldwide, but only 17 in the United States. The red-tailed hawk, described in this story, is one of the most prevalent of U.S. hawk species. It is fascinating that, even from the same field, some hawks migrate south for the winter, while some remain behind. During this migration period, those drifting south often have to fight battles with local hawks for roosting space. Hawks who migrate waste hundreds of hours and countless amounts of energy just in flying south. Those who remain have to endure bitter, frozen winters.

Do you think this partial migration is an advantage or a disadvantage for the ecosystem? For the species of hawks? (*Partial hawk migration is essential for the ecosystem. If all hawks fled, rabbits, mice, and other rodents would overpopulate during the winter and over-stress the meager stock of winter food. If all the hawks stayed, there wouldn't be enough food for them and many would starve. The system benefits hawks by avoiding excessive competition for food and by ensuring that, no matter what happens during the unpredictable winter period, a strong population of hawks will survive to see a new spring and summer.*)

In this story, a hawk climbs to well over 1,000 feet before beginning her attack dive. Why do hawks attack from such great heights? Why not begin the attack at a height of 100 feet, much closer to the prey? (*There are two reasons. First, hawks soar at great heights to avoid being spotted by potential prey on the ground below. Second, hawks use gravity to power their attacks. They need to fall a great distance to develop the speed they need for a successful surprise attack.*)

Hawks, like most other predators, are territorial. Hawks will aggressively drive off intruding hawks, even those just passing through. Short of actual combat, which is dangerous for both hawks, how do hawks warn, threaten, and try to intimidate other hawks? (*Hawks use body stance and posture, voice, and movement, just as humans do. Hawks flex their wings and glare at each other. They screech a distinctive warning cry, as if threatening, "Don't you dare!" They fly with slow, steady wing beats straight at an intruder. Hawks will use these scare tactics long before resorting to an actual fight.*)

Here are some questions you can research about red-tailed hawks in the library and on the Internet:

1. Some hawks migrate south. Some stay behind. Make lists of as many advantages and disadvantages of both staying and going as you can identify.

2. Hawks get no help from parents once they are able to fly. From that moment on, they're on their own to survive or die. Do you think this is a good system of rearing the next generation? Why do you think hawks use it? Research as many advantages as you can of this system. What does it do for the young hawks who survive? What does it do for the older hawks? What does it do for the species as a whole?

Additional Reading

Here are references for information about hawks and meadow ecosystems. See your librarian for additional titles available at your local library.

Arnold, Caroline. *Hawk Highway in the Sky*. San Diego, CA: Harcourt Brace, 1987.

Austine, G. *The World of the Red-tailed Hawk*. Philadelphia: J. B. Lippincott, 1964.

Callahan, Philip. *The Magnificent Birds of Prey*. New York: Holiday House, 1974.

Eastman, John. *Birds of Forest, Yard, and Thicket*. Mechanicsburg, PA: Stackpole Books, 1997.

Hamerstrom, Frances. *Harrier, Hawk of the Marshes*. Washington, DC: Smithsonian Institution Press, 1986.

Harwood, Michael. *The View from Hawk Mountain*. New York: Charles Scribner's Sons, 1973.

Matteson, Sumner. *Hawks*. Milwaukee, WI: Gareth Stevens, 1995.

McCoy, J. *Lords of the Sky*. New York: Bobbs Books, 1963.

Olsen, Penny. *Falcons and Hawks*. New York: Facts on File, 1992.

Ritchie, Rita. *The Wonder of Hawks*. Milwaukee, WI: Gareth Stevens, 1996.

Russell, Franklin. *Hawk in the Sky*. New York: Holt, Rinehart & Winston, 1965.

Terres, John. *Flashing Wings*. Garden City, NY: Doubleday, 1968.

Deadly "Pray"

Praying Mantis of North America

At a Glance

When we think of deadly dangers and predators, we think *big*. But one of the deadliest hunters on earth is really quite small. Praying mantises occupy a unique position among insects. Maybe it is their thoughtful, inquisitive look, or the way they twist their heads in a knowing, alien, and very un-insect-like way, that makes them seem so different. Maybe it's the giant size of their eyes. Every time humans study these insects, we come away feeling that the praying mantis is a comrade on the journey of exploration, a wise and thoughtful being we'd like to know and with whom we'd want to share philosophies.

It is a shock to realize that the praying mantis is the most relentless and ruthless, the fiercest and greediest hunter on earth. Mantises stalk and devour everything even close to their own size, including other mantises, their own brothers and sisters, their own mates.

Still, humans have always thought of praying mantises as special. In Africa it was believed that mantises could bring the dead back to life if they so chose. Some oriental cultures believed that if a mantis landed on a person, that person was favored by the heavens and should be considered a saint. People in seventeenth-century France believed praying mantises could (and would) point out the correct way home to any lost child.

The term *mantis* comes from the Greek word meaning "prophet," or "clairvoyant." Early American colonists believed mantises were supernatural because they appeared to spend so much time praying.

In truth, if mantises pray, it is only for their next victim and meal. We should be glad praying mantises are small. If they were bigger, they would rule the earth.

"Deadly 'Pray' "

The high school football team had just finished warm-up calisthenics and had started blocking and tackling practice. The crash of helmets and the slap of shoulder pads resounded like sharp thunderclaps across the practice field. Coaches' whistles blew and players grunted and yelled as they struggled to maintain their blocking assignments.

At the far end of the field, a squad of cheerleaders romped and bounced through their routines wearing brightly colored outfits, like splotches of brilliant fall foliage against the solid green of the field. Beyond them the marching band struggled to keep in time and on key as they stumbled through their half-time formations.

Beyond the band stood a solid line of trees, marking the boundary of the school grounds. Gone was the soft summer rustle of supple green leaves. Now the rustling leaves took on a harder, crinklier tone as they began to dry toward the brilliant hues of fall. Instead of a soothing summer lullaby, the leaves seemed to crackle out a warning of impending winter.

Beyond the trees lay thick brambles, then tall reeds lining a small pond. Beyond the pond, a lush meadow spread across a small rise, basking in the late afternoon September sun. Birds sang. Butterflies twitted from meadow flower to flower.

But in that meadow stalked, pound-for-pound, the deadliest, most voracious predator on earth.

From *Close Encounters with Deadly Dangers*. © 1998 Kendall Haven. Libraries Unlimited. (800) 237-6124.

A caterpillar, now thick and long after a summer's feasting, crawled along a stem on a promising bush. Covered with the fuzz of countless hairs, rhythmically moving its rows of tiny legs and feet, the caterpillar inched toward a cluster of juicy leaves. The caterpillar's appetite had grown as the nights became chilly, marking an oncoming change of seasons. It had become an eating machine, turning the green of leaves into fat stores that would last it through a winter of metamorphosis in its cocoon.

The caterpillar hesitated at a Y-shaped split in the branch. Its short feelers groped down both twig-sized limbs. Its smell receptors sensed that the path to the left promised a thicker reward of leaves. Twisting its body in that direction, it began the last few inches of its crawl toward the needed food. It was the last decision the caterpillar would ever make.

It felt the gentle breeze bristle through its fine hairs. It felt the warmth of the sun, about to dip behind the trees and cast the meadow into shadow.

The caterpillar paused at the first leaf and lifted its head. Feelers twitching in the air, it searched for the sounds or smells that would signal a predator and danger. There was no hint of movement or sound nearby. The way was clear for the caterpillar to eat. It dropped its head and, like a lawn mower, began to gobble a wide strip through the leaf.

But the caterpillar was not safe. Anyone could have missed it easily and would have thought it only another twig hanging from the slim branch above. It was colored like a twig. It hung like a twig. It was shaped like a twig. Then its head moved, shifting slightly, turning to aim straight at the caterpillar. The movement was too subtle for the caterpillar to notice.

Again the head turned, dipping first to the left and then slightly to the right, measuring the size of this caterpillar meal, calculating its direction and speed of movement, measuring the distance to within a tiny fraction of an inch.

Nothing else on this killer moved. Its four hind legs rooted it to the branch. Its longer, thicker front legs were folded and held in front of its head, looking exactly like a person with hands folded in prayer.

Again the head rocked, recalculating the distance to attack. And an odd-looking head it was. This was a triangular head with a great bulbous eye, which seemed far too large for the head, bulging from

From *Close Encounters with Deadly Dangers*. © 1998 Kendall Haven. Libraries Unlimited. (800) 237-6124.

each upper corner. It seemed to stare inquisitively at the world, looking far more curious than hungry. Its stare looked friendly and pious, like someone trustworthy, not at all like a vicious killing machine. The praying mantis's head was reminiscent of intelligent, thoughtful aliens in many space movies.

Remarkably, the head of the praying mantis is the only head in the insect world that can turn and swivel left and right, up and down. A praying mantis's head is far more flexible than a human's head and can even turn to glance backward over its shoulder and thin, streamlined body.

This was an ordinary Chinese praying mantis, one of three imported species that have joined the 17 native varieties of mantis in the United States. The Chinese mantis is now one of the most populous varieties in this country. At just over four inches long, this mantis was average sized for an adult. Still, it was no match for some of the tropical varieties of mantis, which reach 10 inches in length and can prey on small rodents and other mammals.

Stiller than a wooden twig the mantis hung, waiting, calculating. Unaware, the caterpillar continued to eat its way along one edge of the leaf, countless tiny legs each scurrying in turn to keep up with the mouth's steady progress.

Quicker than the blink of an eye the mantis struck. Faster than eyes can record, its front arms unfolded and snapped forward. These front two legs also seemed ungainly and disproportionately large on the mantis. Like the front claws on a lobster, these legs had grown thick and powerful. The front two muscular sections (the tibia and femur) were covered with horny, tooth-like spines that could grab and hold any prey, locking it in a vice-like grip.

The twig became an attacking monster. Before the caterpillar was even aware of the danger, both of the mantis's front legs had flashed out, both tibia had snapped back, closing against the femurs like the two parts of a jackknife slamming closed.

The three-inch-long caterpillar was securely trapped in the mantis's grip. The desperate caterpillar, weighing twice as much as the mantis, squirmed and writhed, flexing its powerful body violently from side to side, trying to throw off its attacker. But the spines on the mantis's legs pierced into the caterpillar's soft flesh and would not let go.

From *Close Encounters with Deadly Dangers*. © 1998 Kendall Haven. Libraries Unlimited. (800) 237-6124.

In another blink the caterpillar was jerked up to the mantis's powerful grinding, cutting mandibles (teeth-like mouth parts) and the feast began.

Almost before it started, the attack was over. The caterpillar had been devoured and was gone.

The mantis paused to clean and groom itself like a satisfied kitten. Its head twisted and turned so that its mandibles could slowly nibble down each leg, cleaning away dirt, debris, and any trace of the caterpillar. It rubbed its powerful legs together, as if to dry them. It brushed forward its antennae with its front legs, to lick and clean them with its swiftly nibbling mandibles.

Always the head rocked and rolled in a very intelligent and knowing way. This was early autumn and, having passed through all of its skin sheddings, or molts, this praying mantis was a full-grown adult. Even though it had just eaten a caterpillar weighing more than it did, it was still hungry. Nature has never produced a more voracious eater than a praying mantis.

Spreading its dragonfly-like wings, the mantis buzzed down from the bush, swooping toward the reeds along the pond's shore. Landing near the base of some thick reeds, it climbed to hang invisibly among the brown stalks.

Its head slowly twisted to allow its cavernous, compound eyes to search the area for likely prey. Like flies' eyes, each of the mantis's eyes produces hundreds of pictures of the scene around it. When newly hatched, the mantis preyed on aphids, flies, and mosquitoes. As it grew, it added caterpillars, house flies, butterflies, and ladybugs to its diet. Now, as a full-grown adult, no member of the insect world could withstand its attack. Crickets, grasshoppers, flies, spiders, bees, and wasps all fell victim to the mighty praying mantis. So did smaller mantises. Nothing was safe from this killer.

An adult praying mantis is both fearless and feisty. Unlike a shark, which looks for an *easy* meal, a mantis goes after *every* meal, with scant regard for risks and dangers.

The mantis froze, staring at a small frog sitting in the mud below. The frog had been staring up at the mantis since it first climbed the reed stalk. While frogs regularly feast on mantises, large mantises have been known to attack small frogs, and occasionally to win the fight.

From *Close Encounters with Deadly Dangers.* © 1998 Kendall Haven. Libraries Unlimited. (800) 237-6124.

The mantis now studied the frog, slowly tilting its head to measure size, direction, and distance. But the frog was also studying the mantis, seeing not a predator, but a tasty meal, if only the mantis would edge lower down the stalk and within range of its sticky tongue.

Head steadily bobbing left and right, the bold and hungry mantis edged lower, its four back legs inching down the stalk. The frog waited, Adam's apple slowly bobbing as its tongue prepared to leap after its dinner.

Almost imperceptibly the distance between the two stalking predators narrowed as they stared into each other's eyes like gun fighters on an Old West frontier street. The buzzing of other insects and the rustling of leaves seemed to fade into the distant background as all the pond watched this deadly confrontation.

In a blinding flash both fighters unleashed their weapons. Mantis legs lashed forward just as the frog's tongue shot out. The tongue found and wrapped around one of the front legs. That leg slammed closed over the tongue. The other mantis leg snapped closed over the frog's body just behind its head.

Both were trappers; both were trapped. As both strained to reel in their victim and gain the upper hand, the mantis crashed down on top of the frog. Both struggled in this desperate wrestling match, flipping end-over-end across each other in the mud.

Just as the mantis's mandibles locked onto the frog's back and began to chew, the frog's tongue dragged one mantis leg into its own mouth.

Simultaneously reacting to the pain of attack, both released their grip and sprang back, still fiercely eyeing each other. The mantis lifted its wounded leg to preen and soothe the hurt like a puppy that has stepped on a thorn. The frog twisted its neck and tried to ease the burning in its shoulder.

With a final defiant twist of its head the praying mantis retreated from the battleground, not defeated, but certainly not willing to risk further injury in pursuing this meal.

The meadow and pond were rich with food, and the pickings were easy for a powerful mantis. Besides, its eyes were already locked onto a nearby spider patiently waiting at the edge of its web.

———

From *Close Encounters with Deadly Dangers*. © 1998 Kendall Haven. Libraries Unlimited. (800) 237-6124.

Thinking About This Ecosystem

Praying mantises are part of the insect world that forms a major, but almost invisible, part of every ecosystem. Inventory the insects in your ecosystem. In an open space near your house mark out a 10-x-10-foot square. Try to make a careful inventory of the insects you find inside that square. Don't forget to include flying insects above your square.

Compare your inventory with your classmates'. Did the insect population density and makeup vary with the type of vegetation? That is, did it matter if the square was marked out over mowed lawn, wild grass, in a meadow, by a creek, by a pond, in the woods, or in a field?

Did you find any insect predators in your square? (*Most common insect predators are other insects such as spiders, praying mantises, ladybugs, etc.*) Make a list of the predators you found. Besides insect predators, what animals prey on insects? Use the library and the Internet to research predators of insects. (*Your list should include frogs, birds, lizards, and mammals such as anteaters and chimpanzees, among many others. How many can you find?*)

Thinking About This Predator

Praying mantises are hatched in cluster sacks containing hundreds of eggs. Within moments after struggling to the outside of their hanging egg case, mantises are hungry and ready to eat. The greatest danger for a newly emerging mantis is that its brothers and sisters that hatched minutes before will eat it before it is strong enough to defend itself. In this case, the early "bird" definitely gets the worm. Often more than half of the praying mantises in the last half of an egg cluster to emerge will be eaten by those in the first half to emerge.

Mantises can be found in almost every tropical to temperate ecosystem in the world. Their skin forms a hard, shell-like exoskeleton. As the mantis grows, this rigid shell is outgrown and must be shed. A praying mantis endures five or six such molts, or skin sheddings, as it grows over the three months of summer. On its final molt, it emerges with full adult body and, for the first time, wings.

Here are some questions you can research about praying mantises in the library and on the Internet:

1. Praying mantises are cannibalistic. They will eat anything, including other mantises. What other predator species are cannibalistic? Can you find any advantages to being cannibalistic? What are the disadvantages? Why do you think praying mantises have evolved to be such aggressive cannibals?

2. What makes praying mantises so effective and efficient as hunters and killers? Research as many reasons for their success as you can find.

Additional Reading

Here are references for information about praying mantises. See your librarian for additional titles available at your local library.

Arnett, Ross. *American Insects: A Handbook of the Insects*. New York: Van Nostrand Reinhold, 1985.

Conklin, Gladys. *Praying Mantis, the Garden Dinosaur*. New York: Holiday House, 1978.

Earle, Olive. *Praying Mantis*. New York: Morrow Junior Books, 1969.

Hess, Lilo. *The Praying Mantis, Insect Cannibal*. New York: Charles Scribner's Sons, 1971.

Johnson, Sylvia. *Mantises*. Minneapolis, MN: Lerner Publications, 1985.

Lavies, Bianca. *Backyard Hunter: The Praying Mantis*. New York: Dutton Children's Books, 1995.

Metcalf, Robert. *Destructive and Useful Insects*. New York: McGraw-Hill, 1993.

Phillbrick, Helen. *The Bug Book*. Charlotte, VT: Garden Way Publications, 1974.

Price, Peter. *Insect Ecology*. New York: John Wiley, 1975.

Stefoff, Rebecca. *Praying Mantis*. Vero Beach, FL: Marshall Cavendish, 1997.

Swan, Lester. *Beneficial Insects*. New York: Harper & Row, 1964.

Grizzly Tales

Grizzly Bears of Alaska

At a Glance

Of all bears, the grizzly, officially one of the brown bears, stands alone for its power and ferocity. Grizzlies were revered by many Native American tribes for their bravery and power, and were worshipped by some. It was always grizzlies, not other brown bears or black bears, that stirred the imagination of settlers and the blood of hunters.

In the early 1800s grizzlies ranged across all of what is now the United States as far south as northern Mexico. There were tens of thousands of grizzlies in California alone. Then the repeating rifle was invented. By 1902, the last California grizzly had been killed. By 1930, grizzlies existed only in protected national parks and forests in Montana, Wyoming, the Pacific Northwest, and the wilds of Alaska and Canada. There are now fewer than 50,000 grizzlies left on this continent.

"Grizzly Tales"

The salmon swam hard, desperately hard. Every muscle ached. After four years of living in the ocean's salt water, the fresh water of Alaska's Chitina River burned its gills and was slowly killing the mighty fish. But the salmon didn't care. The scent of its spawning ground was too strong now, and drove the fish on like a cruel whipmaster.

This salmon, like many others racing with it, was born next to a rocky bank in a bend of a small tributary that fed the Chitina River. After living four months in the river's fresh water, an internal alarm clock called the fish to the sea. The salmon spent the next four years happily swimming through the endless blue of the Pacific Ocean, passing Hawaii and drifting as far south as Australia.

Then a second alarm turned on, one that frantically called this female salmon home. Forgetting all else, the salmon began a 5,000-mile journey back to the same bank where she had hatched, this time to lay her own eggs and begin the cycle once again. She had only the faintest scents to guide her on this trek. But now, swimming up the Chitina River, the unique scent of her own tributary was overwhelmingly strong.

Even though she had lost weight during this exhausting voyage, she was still a big fish, over three feet long and weighing 18 pounds. And she was powerful, even in her weakened state. She regularly leapt over low falls and rapids, hurling her body out of the water for five or six feet over rocks. No obstacle was too great for her to overcome to return to the site of her beginning.

Rounding a bend in the narrowing river, the salmon felt swirling turbulence in the water. It signaled another set of rocks to leap over. Backing slightly, she slammed her tail against the current with all her

From *Close Encounters with Deadly Dangers.* © 1998 Kendall Haven. Libraries Unlimited. (800) 237-6124.

might, hurtling forward. At the last second she flipped into the air, arching her tail, hoping to sail over the obstacle.

But a shaggy brown paw with five long, black claws whistled through the air and slammed into the flying salmon. The fish was tumbled high above the stream, twisting its body to regain balance. A dark, shaggy monster, bigger than river boulders, rose up and snatched the fish in its mouth, locking it tight in powerful jaws.

This salmon would not survive to lay her eggs. But the female grizzly bear had caught another meal.

This nine-year-old grizzly was big and nimble for a female. She weighed almost 600 pounds and, because this was early October, was gaining weight fast. Her bushy coat was light brown with gray or silver tips, giving her fur a "grizzled" appearance. This appearance gave grizzlies their name. Grizzlies, close cousins of the Kodiak bear, are part of the brown bear family, one of only eight bear species on earth. The only other North American bears are black bears and polar bears.

The grizzly lumbered to shore with a hopping gate, splashing through the shallow, icy water, still holding her catch tight in her mouth. She was a good fisherwoman, as are most grizzlies. Some waited on shore, reaching out with either paw or mouth to snag passing fish. Some "snorkeled" after fish, dropping their faces under water to rummage after their catch. This grizzly hated to snorkel. No grizzly likes to get its ears wet, but this female *hated* it. Her fishing technique was to wade into the river and stand motionless, waiting for unsuspecting fish to swim too near.

So far during this several-week-long salmon catching season she had snared over 400 salmon. Among the eight grizzlies who had gathered to fish at this spot in the river, great mounds of fish bones and discarded parts littered the shore.

The female grizzly sat on the graveled shore, her long hind legs stretched straight out in front of her. Holding this latest catch between her paws, she eagerly devoured the meal. But still she felt hungry. Since her own internal alarm clock had gone off, she always felt hungry.

Grizzlies, more than any other predator, are driven by the call of the seasons. But then grizzlies aren't true carnivores. Their diet is 75 percent berries, nuts, roots, tubers, and leaves. While grizzlies do

From *Close Encounters with Deadly Dangers*. © 1998 Kendall Haven. Libraries Unlimited. (800) 237-6124.

have sharp, ripping canine teeth, most of their teeth are flat molars for grinding plant food.

Every season has a unique rhythm for a grizzly. April thaws called the grizzly to end her hibernation. Spring was a time to explore, to play, and to scavenge. Grizzlies prefer finding dead meat to having to hunt. Winters are hard in Alaska, and many weak or old elk, deer, caribou, and oxen die during harsh storms. Their slowly rotting bodies are a succulent spring treat for a grizzly.

Standing outside her cave, the grizzly had breathed deeply the smells of spring, her head rocking in a great *U* to test the scents on the wind. Every grizzly has a superb sense of smell. The grizzly's eyesight was poor, and her hearing was only decent, but her nose could pinpoint a passing animal several miles away.

She needed 25 to 30 pounds of food each day in the spring. Winter carcasses and the human garbage dump were plentiful supplies, so there was still plenty of time for snow sliding. Grizzlies love to snow slide more than people like to ski.

The summer was different. The summer was a time of leisure, of digging, and of mating fights.

Grizzlies differ from other bear species in having a great hump of muscle across the top of their shoulders. It gives grizzlies incredible power in their front legs and makes them one of the world's best diggers. Grizzlies dig like steam shovels and can dig up a tunnel faster than a fleeing mole can create it.

In summer, fields are filled with tasty flowers and with mice, squirrels, and gophers to dig out and eat. Boulders can be overturned to reveal wiggling masses of tasty insects.

Grizzlies don't need as much food in the summer—only 10 pounds or so a day. So life was leisurely and good for the grizzly in the sun-drenched meadows and lush woods. Maybe this is because she was a female and didn't have to survive ferocious mating fights. This female mated in July and would give birth during her hibernation this winter. But the great male she mated with, a hulking, 1,300-pound monster with jet-black fur beneath his silver tips, had to survive two brutal fights to win the privilege.

There are no preliminaries to a grizzly fight. They do not circle each other and growl threats. To circle shows hesitation and fear. A grizzly comes straight in, and in a blink, like a thunderclap on a clear blue day, the two bears are at each other's throats. They box, claw,

From *Close Encounters with Deadly Dangers*. © 1998 Kendall Haven. Libraries Unlimited. (800) 237-6124.

bite, shove, and kick. While its teeth are a grizzly's most dangerous weapons, their sharp, five-inch-long claws (five on each paw) can tear through the thickest fur and deep into an opponent's flesh.

The fights never last more than a few minutes. Both males are usually torn open with great gashes. The fight lasts until one flees in fear of losing his life, or until one has died, unable to escape in time. All male grizzlies are criss-crossed with long, jagged scars from these mating fights.

Then another alarm clock had rung inside the female grizzly's head. Fall was coming. It was time to fatten up before hibernation. The call drove her to add as much as a 10-inch-thick layer of fat during the fall, increasing her body weight by a third.

Now the grizzly needed 80 pounds of food a day. When the salmon had started to run up the rivers to spawn, the female had lumbered to the shore to stuff herself with fish.

But the salmon run was ending. She had caught only six salmon all day. It was time to search elsewhere. Seven other grizzlies had gathered at the river. Now they, too, began to drift away, for the fall was a time to eat at a non-stop, frenzied pace.

Grizzlies aren't territorial. Certainly there had been squabbles at the river and the biggest males got the best fishing spots, but a grizzly doesn't mind if others wander into its home territory. When they gathered to eat at the river and at the human garbage dump, grizzlies got along well.

The female lumbered up a thickly wooded slope of spruce and pine, loping on her pigeon-toed, flat feet. Bears, like humans, walk on their heels instead of their toes, as do most predators.

Gathering clouds overhead held the bleak, dull look of coming snow. The grizzly remembered a thick berry patch over this rise. Grizzlies are very intelligent and remember the location of each of their good catches.

Rummaging through the thorny vines for the last of the sweet berries, the grizzly's stomach told her to eat faster. In the fall, a grizzly thinks of bigger meals and of snaring bigger game.

She remembered a flock of sheep she had found two falls before. She and another female had eaten well for two days before a man with a yelping dog chased them away. She had escaped. The other grizzly had fallen when the man's rifle spat out fire and noise.

From *Close Encounters with Deadly Dangers.* © 1998 Kendall Haven. Libraries Unlimited. (800) 237-6124.

Dangers lurked around sheep, but sheep were filling. As she swung her head in a great *U*, she could smell a flock far down in the valley below.

She loped down the forest slope, across a small stream, and smashed through a flimsy rail fence. Ahead of her, sheep nervously "baaaa-ed" and edged away into a tight circle.

Grizzlies don't stalk. They don't rely on cunning or speed. A grizzly simply lumbers in and attacks. In a flash one sheep was down, held tight in the bear's clutches, and a second limped badly from a wicked swipe by one of her paws. The grizzly knew that sheep wouldn't go far and settled into her feast.

As she finished the first sheep and started for the second, which had collapsed a short distance away, the grizzly heard the sound of coming trouble. It was a human sound, a truck. She rose up on her hind legs, standing a full eight feet tall, to see, hear, and smell better.

A man and dogs were coming. This was not the time to take chances. She was to become a mother this winter.

The grizzly ran for the cover of forest slopes. Though she seemed to lope leisurely along, the grizzly could run at 35 miles per hour.

Reaching the steep slope, she heard the truck stop and two dogs bound out, barking wildly as they took up the chase. She heard a man call after them.

The grizzly climbed swiftly, searching for a place to hide, for a clump of the right-colored bushes where she would be invisible.

The dogs easily found her in her hiding spot, snarling and barking at the thick clump of bushes as they cautiously inched forward.

Still she sat motionless, waiting for them to either leave or inch too close. One of the dogs rushed in, as if to nip at her leg. A huge front paw ripped through bush and air, smashing into the dog's side. The dog yelped in surprise and pain as it was lifted off its feet and thrown 20 feet back, where its crushed body slammed into the soft dirt at the base of a tree.

Whining, the second dog stood over the mangled body of its mate. If he had attacked, it also would have died. If it had run, the grizzly would probably have chased it, as is her natural instinct.

Since the dog did neither, the grizzly turned and galloped away. By the time the man arrived to find his slain dog, the grizzly was half a mile higher up the mountainside and would not be caught.

From *Close Encounters with Deadly Dangers.* © 1998 Kendall Haven. Libraries Unlimited. (800) 237-6124.

Snow flurries swirled across the mountains as she paused to rest. She had been both foolish to venture after sheep and lucky to have escaped so easily. She would stay much higher up in the mountains and content herself with whatever she could scrounge while she prepared her den.

Soon the snows would thicken, turning the ragged mountains into gray, misty shrouds, and she would sleep. Sometime in January, she would wake enough to give birth to twins, each tiny cub born deaf, blind, and weighing only one and one-half pounds. They would sleep with her and feed on her milk until the spring alarm clock called them all out to a new season.

Thinking About This Ecosystem

What do you think defines the ecosystem in which the grizzlies live? (*It is the mountain terrain rather than the vegetation that defines the grizzlies' ecosystem and separates it from other systems.*) Is there a difference between the grizzlies' ecosystem and their habitat? (*Not really. Grizzlies roam freely over all physical parts of their ecosystem. Thus their habitat, where they live, is the entire ecosystem. Before they were killed and driven out of other parts of the continent, grizzlies roamed over a wide variety of ecosystems and ecosystem types.*)

What are the major characteristics of the ecosystem of the grizzlies? (*Major characteristics include mountainous terrain; short summers and long, cold, snowy winters; extensive pine forests; frequent meadows and fields; abundant streams, lakes, and rivers; and minimal permanent human population. What other characteristics can you find?*) Use the library and the Internet to create a list of other mammals that live in this same habitat.

Thinking About This Predator

Adult grizzlies range from six to eight feet, nose to tail, and eight to ten feet tall when standing. Though a member of the brown bear family, the grizzly's coat varies from pale brown through black, with silver tips that create the distinctive grizzly look. One reason a human might want to distinguish brown bears from blacks is that brown bears can't climb trees, while black bears can.

Grizzlies are scavengers first (hence their love of garbage dumps), vegetarians second, diggers for insects and small rodents third, and hunters as a last resort. When do you think a grizzly is most likely to hunt larger game and fish? (*In the fall, when it feels the call to eat, eat, eat to fatten up for winter hibernation.*)

From *Close Encounters with Deadly Dangers*. © 1998 Kendall Haven. Libraries Unlimited. (800) 237-6124.

Grizzlies are the top predator in their ecosystem. What is the surest way to tell which predator is really the top predator? (*Other predators grudgingly give up their own kills to the top predator. They would never do that for some other predator they thought they might be able to defeat in battle. Wolves and even fierce wolverines give way when a grizzly muscles in with a snarling roar and a show of deadly teeth.*)

As fierce as they might appear to be, grizzlies love to play. In spring they snow slide, sitting or standing and sliding down steep slopes. In summer they wrestle, play chase, and splash in rivers and shallow lakes. Which other predators like to play? Which predators don't? (*Of the 17 predators described in this book, seven—hippos, grizzlies, sperm whales, lions, Arctic wolves, tigers, and hawks to some extent—do play. The other ten—anacondas, army ants, piranhas, sharks, scorpions, praying mantises, crocodiles, cobras, squids, and Komodo dragons—do not. Add to these lists other predators you have read about.*)

Grizzlies display a strong homing instinct. They may wander, but always return to the same home range, or territory. They are not very territorial or defensive about this home range, however. Other grizzlies are allowed to drift in to feed or rest for a few days. Grizzlies are rarely involved in the territorial battles that other species so often have. Can you think of reasons why grizzlies might not be as territorial as some other species?

Here are some questions you can research about grizzly bears in the library and on the Internet:

1. Grizzly bears have been driven out of northern Mexico, all of the United States (where they used to flourish) and most of Canada. What does a population of grizzly bears need to survive as a stable population?

2. Grizzly cubs are raised exclusively by their mother. Their father plays no role in their rearing, protection, and training. Make lists of predator species in which (1) the father plays a significant role in child rearing and protection, (2) the father is simply uninvolved, and (3) the father is an active danger and threat to his offspring. Try to find advantages and disadvantages of each system.

Additional Reading

Here are references for information about grizzly bears and the mountain forest ecosystem. See your librarian for additional titles available at your local library.

Annixter, Jane, and Paul Annixter. *The Year of the She-Grizzly.* New York: Coward-McCann, 1978.

Betz, Dieter. *The Bear Family.* New York: Tambourine Books, 1982.

Calabro, Marian. *Operation Grizzly Bear.* New York: Four Winds Press, 1979.

Craighead, Frank. *Track of the Grizzly.* San Francisco: Sierra Club Books, 1987.

Hanna, Warren. *The Grizzlies of Glacier.* Missoula, MT: University of Montana Press, 1978.

Haynes, Bessie. *The Grizzly Bear: Portraits from Life.* New York: Dodd, Mead, 1992.

Lepthien, Emile. *Grizzlies.* New York: Childrens Press, 1996.

Mentl, Jerolyn. *The Grizzly.* Mankota, MN: Baker Street Productions, 1981.

Patent, Dorothy. *The Way of the Grizzly.* New York: Clarion Books, 1987.

Peacock, Doug. *Grizzly Years.* New York: Henry Holt, 1995.

Potts, Steven. *The Grizzly Bear.* Mankato, MN: Creative Education, 1997.

Schnaider, Bill. *Where the Grizzly Walks.* Missoula, MT: Mountain Press Publications, 1977.

Schoomaker, Walter. *The World of the Grizzly Bear.* Philadelphia: J. B. Lippincott, 1978.

Weaver, John. *Grizzly Bears.* New York: Dodd, Mead, 1982.

Ḣowl of the Ḣunt

Wolves of the Canadian Arctic Tundra

At a Glance

Wolves have always been magical but terrifying creatures for humans. Little Red Riding Hood, the Three Little Pigs, and Peter all met the embodiment of their greatest fears and dangers in a wolf. Romulus and Remus, the warlike founders of Rome, were raised by a wolf. Wolves are gray creatures of the twilight, with yellow, slanted eyes and an eerie, bone-chilling howl that sounds strangely human.

Wolves have been thought to appear magically out of the shadows when someone is lost, in trouble, and alone. Their tendency to prey on the sick, the weak, and the defenseless adds to their evil mystique.

Wolves seem to represent the most animalistic, brutal, uncontrollable parts of humans. In fiction, when humans turn evil at midnight under a full moon, they turn into werewolves. The Latin word for wolf, *lupulla*, means "witch." In Germany, witches ride on wolves and sometimes turn into wolves.

103

Real-world wolves are cold-weather animals that achieved their greatest development during the ice ages when North America and Europe were either buried in ice and snow or covered with tundra-like, sparse vegetation. Timber wolves and other, warmer-weather species of wolves still roam through the northern reaches of the United States. But as the world has warmed over the past centuries, Arctic wolves, the northernmost of all wolves, have been reduced to the northern fringes of Canada and Alaska, and on scattered Arctic islands.

"Howl of the Hunt"

The female wolf hunched her back to the biting wind that gusted out of the northwest, and momentarily closed her eyes as she yawned. She was a two-year-old Arctic wolf and thus in her last year of youth. Streaks of gray played through her snow-white winter coat. Soon shades of brown and dark gray would appear as she shed her heavy fur with the June thaw.

It was mid-morning in early May. Before her stretched miles of open tundra, extending farther than eyes could see or legs could walk over flat plains, low rolling hills, and occasional, jagged ridge lines. Above her stretched a sapphire sky with only a few traces of white clouds near the far-off horizon. Caribou were beginning to return from the south in herds so large she could hear and feel the pounding of their hooves from miles away.

Soon birds and geese would return in great flocks, chirping and honking. In mid-summer, black flies and mosquitoes would buzz in thick clouds over the bogs of spongy moss and standing water. But now, between gusts of wind, not a single sound drifted through the crystal-clear air. It was a magnificent world of total silence, at least until the four pups woke from their nap and wanted to play.

Through long winter months the pack had roamed through quick, twilight days and across endless dark-gray nights, lit by the roving curtains of the Northern Lights, searching for food, sleeping curled up in hollows in the drifting snow. Now it was spring and the pattern of life had changed. The dominant female, the leading female of the pack, had become pregnant and built a den for her cubs.

The wolves had halted their wandering, even though wandering was the basic nature of wolves, and adopted a fixed territory for their

From *Close Encounters with Deadly Dangers.* © 1998 Kendall Haven. Libraries Unlimited. (800) 237-6124.

summer home. They would neither roam nor hunt outside this territory until the pups were strong enough for the rigors of nomadic wanderings, in September. Deep loyalty to the pack is a strong characteristic of the wolf's nature.

This female, actually the pups' aunt, loved to baby-sit while their mother trotted off to hunt. All adult wolves dote over pups, heaping lavish attention and care on each one. Wolves never outgrow their love of play, and there is no better excuse for a romping, rolling game of tag than four, five-week-old pups with sturdy bodies, long, gangly legs they are just beginning to control, and an insatiable appetite for fun.

The "aunt" wolf allowed two of the twelve-pound balls of brown fuzz to chew on the thick fur of one leg until one nipped some skin. Then she growled and snatched her leg away. Both pups scampered toward the den in a rolling, yelping tumble of retreat. In less than a minute they were back, tails wagging so hard their whole back ends shook. One wagged so hard his wobbly back legs collapsed and he happily rolled onto his back, pawing at his sister to play with him.

The wolf bent down and licked the pups, nuzzling her nose against their faces. The other two romped nearby, pouncing on and wrestling with a stick. At the moment, the stick seemed to be winning.

Life was good for this young female wolf in a stable pack. But as she gazed over vast stretches of rock, snow, and frozen tundra, she longed to be the dominant female of her own pack, to claim her own summer territory with *her* mate, to bear her own pups, to allow *others* to baby-sit as she trotted off to hunt, bowing to no one but her mate, the pack leader and most powerful male.

The pups scattered around her had been born in early April, blind, deaf, toothless, and with legs too weak to stand on. In just five weeks they had gained 10 pounds and had grown sharp little teeth that loved to gnaw, and now had solid bodies they could almost control as they romped through their play. By September they would be fierce young wolves, half-grown at 70 or 80 pounds, able to hunt and to cover 50 miles a day as the pack began its endless winter wandering.

The cubs' mother returned, loping leisurely across the rocks and tundra, her shadow streaking out across the bare ground from the sun perched low over the horizon. The baby-sitter turned to make her greeting. Keeping her head submissively low, she wagged her tail.

From *Close Encounters with Deadly Dangers*. © 1998 Kendall Haven. Libraries Unlimited. (800) 237-6124.

The mother barked and snarled, sensing that the younger female harbored resentment and wasn't sincere in her greeting. The baby-sitter rolled onto her back, acknowledging the mother's dominant position, and whined, begging for forgiveness. The mother lapsed into friendly licking. Her tale wagged, too. Within the pack, the bonds between wolves are strong and affectionate, even though they are ever-conscious of rank.

The mother and several males had found a warren of snowshoe hares. They had chased rabbits through the night and early morning, each wolf hunting alone. The mother had caught and eaten two. Food is scarce in the frozen Arctic. A wolf will eat every part of a rabbit, including the skin and fur, even grinding up the bones with its hind teeth and steeltrap-strong jaws.

The mother would now regurgitate much of her catch for her pups. This was the best way to feed pups still too young to travel to a kill site. It kept the meat warm, clean, and fresh until they could eat. Besides, meat was much easier to carry in an extended stomach than dragging a carcass by one's teeth through the rocks, dirt, and snow.

During fall, winter, and spring, the pack depended on herds of caribou and musk oxen for survival. Bringing down animals of that size and strength meant exhaustive, coordinated work and the constant threat of injury.

Every injury to a wolf was life threatening. Injured wolves couldn't effectively hunt. Often they were attacked and killed by their own pack. Always they were outcast and forced to survive alone. Rabbits, squirrels, and summer in general were a welcome relief. During the summer, the fields would overflow with squirrels, hares, mice, and lemmings, and there would be no need to hunt bigger game as a coordinated pack. Each wolf could catch its fill on its own.

The young female hadn't eaten for two days. She would hunt with the pack tonight. Maybe she would catch a rabbit or two herself.

Late in the afternoon the small pack gathered: one young male, three young females, and the dominant pair. They all wagged their tails, heads submissively low for the powerful silver-gray male that led the pack. With neck hair bristling and teeth bared, he issued warning barks and growls at each pack member to remind all of his dominance. These fierce displays maintained a rough and rugged harmony within the pack.

Each wolf was excited to begin the hunt. There was much yelping and yapping, much leaping and rolling. Then one of the wolves

From *Close Encounters with Deadly Dangers.* © 1998 Kendall Haven. Libraries Unlimited. (800) 237-6124.

started the howl. Everyone else stopped playing to join in. All six adult wolves howled in chorus, heads thrown back and mouths wide open, each adopting a different key. If two wolves slid onto the same note, one quickly changed so that the different tones wove together into an eerie, human-like chorus that drifted in shimmering waves across the quiet, frozen landscape. From the far distance a second pack of wolves answered with their own howls. The air filled with waves of the ghostly music and chilled the blood of every mammal on the tundra.

The mother stayed behind with her pups. The other five loped to the hunt in single file. The dominant male trotted in the middle, his tail up to show his rank. The young male led, his nose riding just above the frozen ground as he searched for some trace scent to follow. The baby-sitter conjured images of fresh rabbit or maybe sweet caribou meat in her head as she followed in the rear of the line.

The sun set at 10:00 P.M. It would rise again in five hours. The young male in the lead slowed, sniffing louder, then turned left toward a small rise, his tail wagging.

Soon he turned, yapping and bouncing, his tail wagging so hard it punished the air, thrashing like a desperate windshield wiper in his excitement.

He had found a fresh trail.

The dominant male sniffed the trail: musk ox, very fresh, traveling slow. Then he yapped his command. They would hunt musk ox tonight. The young female softly moaned. Musk oxen were the hardest of all big game to bring down and the most likely to injure one of the hunters.

The pack's steady lope soon became a gallop as they raced after their prey.

Over the rise they spotted the oxen, a herd of 50 drifting slowly northward.

Wolves do not stalk their prey for a surprise attack as would a lion or tiger. There is no cover in the tundra to slink through.

The wolves use a different plan. Two veering left, three veering right, they circled wide around the small herd, like fence posts in a moving corral. Around and around they galloped, closing slowly, tightening their grip on the oxen.

The oxen shifted into defensive position. The males formed a circle, facing out, shoulder to shoulder, with females, children, and

From *Close Encounters with Deadly Dangers*. © 1998 Kendall Haven. Libraries Unlimited. (800) 237-6124.

the old and sick hiding inside. Each male musk ox weighed four to six times what a grown wolf weighs. Each ox had wide-set, pointed horns. Each had powerful hind hooves and legs. Working together, five wolves *might* bring down one of the great males, but several were sure to be badly injured in the process.

The wolves wanted nothing to do with the males. It was the young and the sick they were after. But they needed to get *past* the males to reach them.

Around and around danced the wolves, inching closer to the herd on every lap. On a signal from the dominant male, all five wolves charged toward one group of male oxen, their teeth bared, ears pinned back, hot breath streaming into the black night as mini-clouds that instantly froze to tiny ice crystals and then evaporated into the cold black sky.

The point of the charge was not to engage the males, but to create confusion and panic. If they were lucky, a charge would open a hole in the males' circle and let the wolves pass through to the easily killed young beyond.

The first charge failed. The oxen held their ground and lashed their horns side to side to ward off the wolves. The second charge failed as well. The wolves could hear the nervous stomping and bleating of the young behind the massive male barrier, and yapped and howled as they circled to drive those young and sick oxen into a panicked frenzy.

On the third charge, one great male bolted forward to attack the young male wolf. The wolf's claws and paws sprayed snow as he skidded into a squealing turn to avoid the slashing horns. Two younger male oxen followed the first one forward, bellowing, into the night.

A gap in the defensive ring momentarily opened. Two wolves dashed through this hole to the inner circle of females and young.

Young oxen bleated in terror and stampeded as the wolves darted through their ranks, nipping at heels and muzzles. Confusion and panic reigned. The defensive circle collapsed. Oxen bolted in all directions.

The wolves darted in and out of the thundering mass of oxen and the clouds of dust they raised as they fled. Like expert trail hands on a cattle drive, the wolves cut the herd into smaller and smaller groups, testing the speed and strength of each ox they passed, searching for the weak and the slow.

From *Close Encounters with Deadly Dangers*. © 1998 Kendall Haven. Libraries Unlimited. (800) 237-6124.

Two of the wolves isolated an old male with a lame foot.

One wolf leapt at the haunches of this old, exhausted ox whose wheezing breath and white, terror-filled eyes made it clear he was too tired to resist. The wolf nipped at the ham string muscle and bounded back to avoid the ox's hooves as they lashed out with the power to splinter rock.

A second wolf sprang at the ox's muzzle, locking onto its snout as a diversion for the real attack. The baby-sitter and the dominant male raced in on the same side and crashed into the ox's rump.

It stumbled and bucked sideways, struggling to keep its balance. A fourth wolf darted in to bite and tear an Achilles tendon in the ox's lower leg. The last wolf jumped at the ox's face, slashing at its eyes to keep it from properly reacting to the real attack behind.

Hurt, confused, and disoriented, the ox slipped on its injured back leg and sprawled to the ground. All five wolves dove to attack the now defenseless prey.

Wolves have neither the size nor the power to kill quickly as a lion does. The wolves' fangs and canine teeth slashed at the ox's throat and tore at its great leg muscles.

The ox bled to death as the rest of the herd nervously regrouped a short distance away, knowing there would be no more attacks this night.

The baby-sitter ate her fill. But inside she felt a deep stirring. This was a good pack, but she wanted to find a mate and create her own family. The pups would soon grow to take her place. Late this summer, while food was still plentiful, she would strike out on her own.

But for now, content, she ate, nuzzled next to the others of her family.

Thinking About This Ecosystem

Arctic tundra is a desert region with scant plant life and correspondingly sparse animal life. The tropical rain forest is just the opposite. It contains the greatest amount and diversity of plant and animal life per acre on earth. Compare the complexity of these two ecosystems. (*Look for information on biomass production per acre, number of plants and animals per acre, number of species per acre, and complexity and number of levels of the food web. See if your research agrees with the common notion that the less prolific the habitat, the simpler the food chain must be.*)

From *Close Encounters with Deadly Dangers.* © 1998 Kendall Haven. Libraries Unlimited. (800) 237-6124.

Which ecosystem, Arctic tundra or tropical rain forest, do you think is more stable? That is, which is better able to resist some radical impact or sudden change? (*This is a much harder question to answer. Common sense would say the rain forest would be much more stable because the food web is so much more diverse. But recent studies have shown the sparse Arctic tundra environment to be extremely stable and resilient. Scientists aren't as sure about the stability of these ecosystems as they were 30 years ago.*)

Do you see any advantage to being a field mouse in the Arctic tundra as opposed to being a field mouse in a meadow in the southeast United States? (*The Arctic field mouse lives in a harsher environment with less food and bitter, cold winters. But the Arctic mouse also has less competition for what food there is, and has far fewer predators to worry about.*)

What role does the wolf play in maintaining a healthy Arctic ecosystem? (*Wolves prey on, or weed out, the weak, the sick, and the old. In this way, only healthy, strong animals survive to pass their genes on to the next generation. The resulting populations of caribou and oxen are heartier and healthier.*)

Thinking About This Predator

Wolves, more than any predator described in this book, bond to their family unit and are strongly affectionate. Wolves form loving, supportive, playful families and mate for life. They hunt together. They wander together. All adults in the family help raise, feed, and train the pups. They defend each other. The power of this family unit has been a key element in their survival. More than almost any other predator, wolves display a strong sense of humor and love to play jokes on other family members.

Can you think of domestic animals whose behavior seems similar to that of wolves? How similar? (*Many dog breeds act similarly to wolves. In his famous stories,* Call of the Wild *and* White Fang, *Jack London blurred the boundary between dog and wolf by having a domestic dog join a wolf pack. Some people have even raised wolves as domestic pets and describe them as affectionate, intelligent, and playful. Raising wolves [as is true for any wild animal] requires special knowledge and space and is not advisable. Still, it has been successfully done on many occasions. Make lists of the characteristics of dogs and wolves that are similar and dissimilar.*)

Wolves can be found in the northern latitudes worldwide. The most common North American wolf is the timber wolf, sometimes called the southern wolf because it lives at the southern fringe of the wolves' domain. See if you can find differences in the behavior, diet, and life-styles of timber wolves and Arctic, or tundra, wolves.

Why do you think a wolf would want to live in the harsh, frozen climate of the Arctic tundra if it could migrate farther south to a more pleasant environment with more abundant food? (*In the Arctic tundra the wolf is the undisputed top predator, with little competition from other wolves or other hunters.*

Arctic wolves also have historically faced no real danger from humans. [This is changing with the modern use of helicopters, snow mobiles, and radar tracking systems for hunters.] Finally, wolves are cold-weather animals. The bitter Arctic environment does not feel as rugged to a wolf as it would to a human.)

Here are some questions you can research about Arctic wolves in the library and on the Internet:

1. Who preys on wolves? What limits Arctic wolf populations?

2. Why are there fewer wolves in the United States and Canada now than there used to be? What do wolves need in order to survive?

Additional Reading

Here are references for information about wolves and the Arctic tundra ecosystem. See your librarian for additional titles available at your local library.

Ballard, W. B., and T. Sparker. *Unit 13 Wolf Studies.* Juneau, AK: Alaska Department of Fish and Game, 1979.

Banfield, A. *The Mammals of Canada.* Toronto: University of Toronto Press, 1974.

Brandenburg, Jim. *To the Top of the World.* New York: Walker, 1993.

Clark, K. *Food Habits and Behavior of the Tundra Wolf on Central Baffin Island.* Toronto: University of Toronto Press, 1971.

Clarkson, Ewan. *Wolf Country.* New York: E. P. Dutton, 1975.

Fiennes, Richard. *The Order of Wolves.* New York: Bobbs-Merrill, 1986.

Fox, M. *Behavior of Wolves, Dogs, and Related Canids.* New York: Harper & Row, 1981.

Harrington, Fred, and Paul Paquet, eds. *Wolves of the World.* Park Ridge, NJ: Noyes Publications, 1982.

Klinghammer, E., ed. *The Behavior and Ecology of Wolves.* New York: Garland, 1979.

Lawrence, R. D. *Wolves.* San Francisco: Sierra Club Books, 1990.

Lopez, Barry. *Of Wolves and Men.* New York: Charles Scribner's Sons, 1978.

Mowat, Farley. *Never Cry Wolf.* Boston: Little, Brown, 1973.

Patent, Dorothy. *Gray Wolf, Red Wolf.* New York: Clarion Books, 1990.

Zimen, E., and L. Boitani. *The Wolf: A Species in Danger.* New York: Delacorte Press, 1981.

"Lion" Around

Lions of Africa's Serengeti Plain: King of Beasts

At a Glance

The lion is often called the "King of the Jungle." But lions do not live in jungles. They live in open savanna grasslands dotted with acacia trees. Lions' behavior is almost the opposite of what humans would consider to be noble and "kingly."

Male lions are lazy. They would rather steal food than hunt their own. Male lions are bullies who don't work, don't help raise their young, rarely hunt (leaving that chore to the females), and don't make any real contribution to the lion pride (the lion family unit). They simply muscle in and take whatever they want: the softest grass and best shade during the heat of the day, the tastiest parts of everyone else's catches.

So why do we call lions "kings?" Because they are the biggest predator in their ecosystem and because their mane creates a regal appearance. Hyenas, cheetahs, wild dogs, jackals, and leopards hunt and kill as efficiently as lions, but lions can overpower every one of these other predators on the African plain and steal their food. Lions are the top niche in the structure of their ecosystem. We have always called the creature in that position "king."

" 'Lion' Around"

The hot red sun eased over the eastern horizon, but only a fuzzy, orange glow reached the ground through a dense layer of fog. Dew clung thick to the grass and soaked the hairs around the young male lion's oversized feet as he padded softly across this 10,000-square-mile savanna grassland. He stopped, head raised, listening, smelling, and then he roared.

His cry was answered by the threatening roars of a nearby pride, announcing that he would not be welcome in their territory.

He lowered his head and trudged on alone. His empty stomach twisted in a painful growl. He had never been this hungry in his young life.

Just south of the African equator and along the northern border of Tanzania, the Serengeti Plain housed the greatest collection of large wildlife on earth. For humans, the local language was Swahili. For animals it was grunts, roars, growls, chirps, and bleating calls. But no cry was listened to more carefully than the roar of hunting lions.

This was early April. The short rainy season was ending. The grass was slowly drying and browning. The herds of countless thousands of wildebeests, gazelles, impalas, and zebras, which arrived in early November with the first rains, were thinning as they migrated west after water and food. Their young had been born. Those that had survived the constant threat of preying jackals, cheetahs, leopards, hyenas, and lions followed their mothers on the dusty trek.

As the fog evaporated around the young lion, he snarled in frustration at two pilot birds hopping through the grass. It had been another bungled night of hunting and now he faced another day of hunger. Already his skin hung loose around him. His ribs had begun to show through his hide.

Why hadn't he paid more attention when the lionesses jogged out to hunt? Why hadn't he watched his mother and sisters more closely? Why had he always felt compelled to play instead of seriously practice his hunting?

Again he snarled. What was *wrong* with chasing his own tail? It was fun. So was pouncing on sticks and beetles. He still liked to do it, even though he knew it was juvenile.

From *Close Encounters with Deadly Dangers.* © 1998 Kendall Haven. Libraries Unlimited. (800) 237-6124.

If only his mother had told him he would be driven out of the pride when he started his third year, and that the adult males would stop ignoring him and fiercely turn on him once his mane began to grow. If only he had known he would become one of the lone, nomadic lions he had laughed at as a cub when the adults in his pride had driven them away. *Then*, then he would have paid more attention while his mother demonstrated proper hunting technique.

The lion shook his mane in bitter frustration. This mane would grow handsomely darker into a chestnut-brown masterpiece as it continued to lengthen and thicken. His body would some day fill out into 450 pounds of muscle to match his now oversized and gangly feet.

He thought back over the failures of this night's hunt, the seventh since he had been driven out to fend for himself. Shortly after complete darkness, when a lion's hunting period was just beginning, he heard the distant, triumphant cries of successful lionesses and the angry squabbling of lions over rights to the kill. It made his desperate hunger and loneliness seem overwhelming.

He spotted a lone gazelle, the perfect meal for a lone lion, the perfect chance to prove his hunting prowess.

Lions hunt primarily with their eyes, as do all cats, and secondarily with their excellent hearing. They have a sense of smell almost as good as a tracking dog, but rarely use it on the hunt.

Instinctively the lion's body dropped into a low crouch as he crept forward, now invisibly blending with the golden grass. His mind flashed through every rule he could remember from hunting with his mother. Circle down wind. Approach slowly in a low, zigzag pattern. Freeze whenever the prey lifts its head. Don't be distracted by passing birds or mice. Don't roll over to scratch an itch or bat your sister. Oh, if only his sister were here to help him now. If only he hadn't turned every hunt into a game, knowing one of the adult lionesses would catch enough to let him eat his fill.

The gazelle paused in its chewing and lifted its head, not in alarm, just in a routine, wary check of its surroundings for signs of danger.

The lion froze. Not a muscle moved, not an eye blinked, not a tail twitched. He breathed silently through open mouth, his hot, stale breath bending the grass like a gentle wind. His shoulder muscles burned with the strain of holding his 300-pound body motionless before the gazelle dropped its head back to the grass, content that all was safe.

From *Close Encounters with Deadly Dangers*. © 1998 Kendall Haven. Libraries Unlimited. (800) 237-6124.

The lion resumed his quiet creeping. He would weigh over 400 pounds in another year, *if* he could catch enough to keep from starving this spring. His growling stomach reminded him that this was a deadly serious hunt, a necessity of survival. For the first time he *felt* like a hunter. *He* was stalking an unaware prey as great lions had for countless centuries. His lips pulled back, baring his deadly teeth. His front claws stretched out to scrape the dirt as he slunk forward.

Closer and closer he crept, his stomach brushing the ground as his powerful legs inched forward. He didn't crawl straight at the gazelle so that it could spot his trail, but rather zigzagged so that he would never be seen.

Forty yards to go, then thirty.

He could hardly stand the nerve-racking tension of his hunt. He wanted to bound forward and announce his terror-inspiring presence with a mighty roar. He hated the waiting of this patient, creeping pace with which his mother had taught him to hunt.

He was almost there. He could already feel his claws leaping through the air to sink into the gazelle's shoulder. Lions do not kill with their fierce claws. Those are used to hold onto the prey while the teeth deliver a killing bite, usually breaking the neck.

He could taste the meat and smell the warm blood of his kill. He could. . . .

Again the gazelle glanced up. Too late the lion froze.

He had been spotted when still 25 yards away!

He had been daydreaming instead of concentrating on his hunt. The gazelle bolted. The lion half-heartedly gave chase. He knew the gazelle had too much of a head start. It sped away at 50 miles per hour.

The lion roared in anger after it.

Why did hunting have to be so hard? It had seemed so easy when he was a bundle of woolly yellow fur, because his mother had done all the work and led him to fresh kills.

As a cub he had loved to scamper after families of warthogs and make them scatter in panic. He had been far too clumsy to catch any of them, but he didn't care. It was fun. Besides, his mother always provided his food.

Where would he find his food now?

Why couldn't he find a half-eaten carcass or a cheetah he could drive away from *its* kill? Lions are opportunists. They will hunt if they

From *Close Encounters with Deadly Dangers.* © 1998 Kendall Haven. Libraries Unlimited. (800) 237-6124.

have to, but would rather scavenge. Jackals and cheetahs can easily be driven off a kill. Every lion learns to watch and follow vultures, the surest guides to recent kills and easy meals.

But the lion could see no vultures, could find no carcasses, nor smaller predators to bully.

Near the end of the night he heard zebras up ahead. Again he tensed. Carefully, he circled downwind so that the zebras would not smell his approach. Carefully he zigzagged closer and closer. He would not fail. Tonight he would eat *zebra*, the favorite meal of every lion.

The blood pounded through his ears. One instinct urged him to creep closer with slow caution, while another screamed for him to attack boldly, fangs bared. He lay in the grass for a moment, deciding.

And then he charged, springing through the final yards of grass like a thundering freight train.

With a snarling growl deep in his throat, he sprang for the nearest zebra, outstretched claws sailing through the final 20 feet of air, reaching toward the kill.

But he had rushed too soon. He still had too far to go. The zebras bolted with amazing quickness. Stretching his claws like a first baseman stretching for a catch, he *did* touch one zebra, raking its shoulder with two claws before he crashed to the ground. His dinner escaped again. The zebra would always carry the scars of the bungled attack, but that was of little comfort to the hungry lion.

By mid-morning, fed or not, lions settle down to nap through the heat of the day. The young lion was too hungry to sleep. He aimlessly wandered under the blue sky and fierce tropical sun, panting to cool himself, thinking only of food and the lost comforts of youth. How he longed to nuzzle up to a familiar lion, rubbing his head against its thick, soft fur. How he craved the reassurance of being licked by another member of his pride, his family.

He spotted a family of warthogs as they emerged from their shallow burrow, a mother and five children. Warthog was hardly the noble meal of a king, but it was better than starving. Swallowing his pride, the lion dropped into a crouch and scurried toward the warthogs.

The desperate lion inched closer to the family as they trotted in line behind their mother, secure in the belief that the heat of the day was adequate protection from the great predator cats of night.

From *Close Encounters with Deadly Dangers*. © 1998 Kendall Haven. Libraries Unlimited. (800) 237-6124.

The lion pounced from his concealment with a thunderous roar. The warthogs scattered, squealing in fright. He sprang first after one runty juvenile, then turned to chase a fatter, older victim. But the warthog disappeared down the entrance of a shallow tunnel before the lion could swat it down with his paw.

The lion roared in rage. He couldn't even catch a warthog!

No! He would not go hungry any longer!

The lion began to dig after his dinner. Sandy savanna dirt sprayed out between his hind legs as his front feet and claws tore away the tunnel's roof.

Five feet, then six feet of warthog tunnel lay exposed. The lion was shamelessly covered in dirt. He caught a glimpse of flesh through the spraying dirt and grass.

He lunged forward. His claws sank into the flesh of warthog rump. He dragged the squealing prey from its hiding place and delivered the killing bite like an expert.

One front paw resting on his first solo kill, the lion lifted his head and bellowed a triumphant roar that echoed over the noontime plain.

This was *his* world, *his* grassland, *his* kingdom. He *would* survive to be king. He had just proved his right to ascend to the throne. Then, for the pure joy of it, he chased his tail before eating.

Thinking About This Ecosystem

We have all seen pictures of the African Serengeti plains. Can you name the major plant and animal species in that ecosystem? (*These elements include grass, grass grazers—rhinos, eland, zebras, waterbucks, hippos, sable, oryx, hartebeests, wildebeests, warthogs, reedbucks, gazelles, impalas, springbucks, and buffalo; trees—acacia and sausage; leaf browsers—giraffes, elephants, bushbucks, and nyalas; predators—lions, hyenas, cheetahs, wild dogs, jackals, foxes, leopards, and crocodiles; and scavengers—birds, and insect recyclers.*)

Are there more grazers and browsers, or predators in this ecosystem? Why? (*There have to be many times more grazers and browsers. One predator will eat many grazers over the course of a year. If the system is to be stable, the grazers must produce as many new animals each year as they lose to predators, disease, and old age combined. That takes a large population.*)

When the dry season comes and the great herds of zebra and gazelles leave, why do they leave, and where do they go? (*The two things grazers need are grass and water. As the grass dries and stops growing, they need new supplies of*

From *Close Encounters with Deadly Dangers.* © 1998 Kendall Haven. Libraries Unlimited. (800) 237-6124.

grass. *As water holes and streams dry up, they must find new sources of water. Grazer herds are on a continual migration chasing water and food.*)

African grazers and browsers face terrible dangers every day from an army of predators. What strategies have they adopted to defend and protect themselves from attack? (*Prey species use a variety of defensive plans. These include* speed—*simply outrun the predators when they attack;* group defense—*10 wildebeests can drive off a lion, whereas one is defenseless;* scentless young—*many newborns have no scent so that predators can't find them;* camouflage—*some species try to blend into the bushes and grass and become invisible to the eyes of roving predators;* large numbers—*if you are one in a herd of a thousand zebras, your odds of surviving are much better than if you wander the plains alone; and* great size—*elephants, rhinos, and hippos are too big to be worth attacking.*)

Thinking About This Predator

Lion cubs are completely dependent on their mothers. Born as three-pound, blind, toothless balls of fur, lion cubs can't even walk for several weeks. Their mother feeds them, protects them, teaches them, and leads them to kills and food for almost two full years before they must become self-sufficient. Male lions develop more slowly than females. Males seem to prefer play to serious practice and training, and have far shorter attention spans. Can you think of other species where males typically develop more slowly than females?

Males do not get serious about their hunting until they are driven out of the pride and forced to become wanderers. Do you think this is a cruel thing to do? What are the advantages for the whole population of lions? (*By allowing the females to remain in the home pride and forcing the males to leave and join some other pride, new blood is regularly brought into the pride, avoiding the dangers of in-breeding. Additionally, the pride keeps from growing too large with too many mouths to feed by driving out all young males. Eventually, nomadic males either find a pride willing to take in a new male, or they snare a female from some pride and start their own. Stable prides seem to have about the same number of adults. A pride with too few males will often accept an outsider. A pride with too many females will often let one go.*)

Lion prides are strongly territorial and will drive out any rogue lion that wanders near their territorial borders. Why do you think they don't welcome strangers to drift through their territory? (*Wanderers will compete with the pride for available local food. Food means survival. A strong pride must drive out other predators to avoid competition and ensure the survival of the pride.*)

Here are some questions you can research about lions in the library and on the Internet:

1. Lion cubs depend on their mothers for every aspect of their survival for the first several years of their lives. Many of the grazer prey species (zebras or impalas, for example) are fully self-sufficient within

hours, or at least days, of birth. Why do you think there is this great difference between these two groups of species?

2. Why do we call lions "the king of the jungle?" Where did that title come from?

Additional Reading

Here are references for information about lions and the African savanna ecosystem. See your librarian for additional titles available at your local library.

Arnold, Caroline. *Lion.* New York: Morrow Junior Books, 1995.

Bender, Lionel. *Lions and Tigers.* New York: Gloucester Press, 1988.

Chipperfield, Mary. *Lions.* Milwaukee, WI: Raintree, 1977.

Hofer, Angelika. *The Lion Family Book.* Saxonville, MA: Picture Book Studio, 1988.

Hoffman, Mary. *Lion.* Milwaukee, WI: Raintree, 1985.

Jackman, Brian. *The Marsh Lions.* Boston: Godine, 1983.

Johnson, Sylvia. *The Lions of Africa.* Minneapolis, MN: Carolrhoda Books, 1977.

National Geographic Society. *Lion Cubs, Growing Up in the Wild.* Washington, DC: National Geographic Society, 1972.

Overbeck, Cynthia. *Lions.* Minneapolis, MN: Lerner Publications, 1981.

Pease, Alfred. *The Book of Lions.* New York: St. Martin's Press, 1987.

Petty, Kate. *Lions.* New York: Gloucester Press, 1990.

Pluckrose, Henry. *Lions and Tigers.* New York: Gloucester Press, 1979.

Schaller, George. *The Serengeti Lion.* Chicago: University of Chicago Press, 1972.

Schaller, George, and Kay Schaller. *Wonders of Lions.* New York: Dodd, Mead, 1977.

Schick, Alice. *Serengeti Cats.* New York: J. B. Lippincott, 1979.

Stone, Lynn. *The Lion.* Vero Beach, FL: Rourke Enterprises, 1989.

Urquhart, Jennifer. *The Big Cats.* Washington, DC: National Geographic Society, 1990.

Yoshida, Toshi. *Young Lions.* New York: Philomel Books, 1984.

Zim, Herbert. *The Big Cats.* New York: Morrow Junior Books, 1975.

Slithering Strikes

Cobras of Southern India

At a Glance

Humans have always been fascinated by poisonous snakes. Cobras, especially, hold a special spot in our nightmares and darkest dreams. However, cobras are far from the most poisonous of snakes. Bushmasters and black mambas, for example, are far more poisonous.

Cobras seem magical because of the way they look at a victim before they strike. Other snakes coil and strike. Only cobras raise their heads high in the air like waving vines or thin tree trunks. Only cobras spread an evil-looking hood at the back of their heads before they attack. Only cobras hiss, sounding like one human "shushing" another. Only cobras dance in the marketplace, waving their hooded heads three or four feet in the air at the command of a snake charmer's flute. Cobras are unique among snakes.

Cobras are the most dangerous snake to humans. Cobras kill more people each year, thousands in China and India alone, than any other snake species. Virtually every one of those deaths occurs at night. The cobra is a nocturnal hunter, slithering through the grass where one can't even see it coming.

"Slithering Strikes"

I was lying on a rock outcropping, my father's rifle at my side, waiting to shoot some wild pigs that had been eating our family's crops. It was night and I fought constantly to stay awake as I lay, waiting for the pigs to return.

My name is Ishani. I am a 16-year-old girl. My family owns a sugarcane farm in the Kerela District along the southern coast of India. Kerela is famous for its wide beaches with broad, curving palm trees. But behind these beaches, steep hills rise toward the mountains. Farms climb these hills where patches of jungle have been cleared away. Our sugarcane field is one of these farms.

We have a wide vegetable garden at the end of the tall rows of waving cane nearest to our house. It was our vegetables that the wild pigs discovered. It was the height of the dry season and food for the pigs was scarce. But if we allowed the pigs to steal from our garden, there would be nothing for us to eat.

Father tried to trap the pigs. We tried to frighten them away with noisemakers. Nothing worked. So my father finally allowed *me* to ambush the pigs at their nest because I am the one who discovered the grass clearing they had trampled into a mattress to sleep on.

This spot lay less than one-quarter-mile from our fields, but it took me 10 minutes to hike here because the undergrowth is so thick in some of the gullies. I had been lying on a blanket among the rocks above the pigs' sleeping spot, hiding since sunset. A full moon hung in the sky. Colors were all soft grays. But the strong moonlight cast the outline of every object clear and crisp.

I heard the distant, soft grunts of pigs and tensed. Here they came!

I also heard a soft rustling through the grass next to my blanket.

It must be a mouse come to sneak a nibble of my sandwich, I thought. I would have kicked at the mouse, but the grunts were coming closer, and I didn't want to alert the pigs to my presence.

The pigs trotted into view, casting hard shadows along the narrow path, a mother and three babies. Slowly, silently, my hand tightened its grip on my father's rifle. I raised it from the blanket.

From *Close Encounters with Deadly Dangers.* © 1998 Kendall Haven. Libraries Unlimited. (800) 237-6124.

At that moment I realized the nearby rustling was too long, too big to be a mouse or rat. It sounded more like . . . like a snake, quietly slithering through the dried grass. I remembered that a cobra had been spotted near here a few weeks ago—not a king cobra (which can grow to 20 feet), but still an 8- or 9-foot monster, the deadliest snake in India.

Many poisonous snakes dash in to nip at you with their fangs. But a cobra actually bites, letting its short fangs sink into your skin. Then it holds on to let the venom flow. It is said that a cobra bite doesn't burn or hurt. It acts like an overdose of anesthetic you get in a hospital operating room. You feel drowsy, peaceful, unafraid, and relaxed. In three minutes you are dead.

Some cobras can spit their venom. From 10 feet they can accurately hit something as small as a human eye. When the poison splashes on your skin it causes terrible burning pain and temporarily blinds you. I have been told that most of these spitting cobras live in Africa. Still, I have never wanted to stand close enough to one of our Indian cobras to find out.

The grunting pigs were below me. But the rustling was *very* close.

I froze, rifle held in mid-air. It *was* a snake, a *big* snake. I could see the soft bands of color on its back in the moonlight. It must be a cobra. My heart pounded so loudly I was sure the snake could hear.

I heard the softly flicking of its tongue. Cobras, like most snakes, gather much of their information about the world through chemical sensors, called receptors, along the roof of their mouths. Their flicking tongues pull in samples of the scents in the air for these receptors to interpret and identify.

My mind knew that cobras strike at movement. I would be safer if I stayed absolutely still. But my feet didn't believe it. They wanted to run.

I heard the snake slither cautiously onto my blanket. I felt its dry skin slide across my bare knee and under the other leg. Eyes squeezed shut, I struggled to suppress a violent shudder. My legs desperately wanted to jump away, kicking wildly at the dreaded snake. I could feel its powerful muscles contract as its skin undulated across my leg.

The cobra seemed to take hours to creep across my legs. It felt at least 50 feet long. All snakes are cold blooded, but this cobra's skin felt warm against my legs as if it had been basking on hot rocks all day.

The muscles of my arm holding the upraised rifle burned with the effort to remain still. But I dared not move.

From *Close Encounters with Deadly Dangers*. © 1998 Kendall Haven. Libraries Unlimited. (800) 237-6124.

I heard the soft plop of the cobra's tail as it dropped past my leg and onto my blanket. The pigs were forgotten. I wanted only to get back to the safety of our family home. As soon as the cobra disappeared into the tall grass, I ran.

Thousands of people are killed each year in India by cobra bites, all during the dark of night, because the cobra is nocturnal. It hunts and eats at night. Cobras mostly eat small meals of rodent, frog, lizard, insect, or bird's egg, and so have to eat often, almost daily. But they can survive months without food if necessary.

In the marketplace snake charmers force their cobras to wake during the day, waving like four-foot-high bamboo poles rising out of their baskets. I have never stayed to watch. I have never wanted to be that close. Cobras are mean and aggressive, and will attack animals (like me) far too large for them to eat, just because the animal happens to be in their way. Cobras don't eat people, they just kill them when they are in the way.

I scrambled into one of the wide gullies I'd have to cross to get back home. I didn't care how much noise I made, as long as I reached the safety of our house and stopped shivering.

Then I heard the rustling behind me, like a soft whisper through the undergrowth. I saw the dry grasses rhythmically wave as something passed invisibly along the ground.

The cobra!

I froze again, pressing my back into the dark shadows along the soft dirt side of the gully. My stomach began to churn and my knees grew weak.

Ten feet from me the cobra stopped. Majestically it raised its head and upper body, three feet, four feet, almost five feet in the air! That meant the snake must be over nine feet long! Its head gently swayed as its shiny, black eyes and flicking tongue surveyed me. I could feel it stare at me and remembered that a cobra's night vision is far better than mine. In terror I realized this cobra stood taller than I did.

I knew it couldn't strike from there, unless it was a spitting cobra. Cobras don't *spring* forward, and so can only strike as far forward as they have raised their heads off the ground. I also knew that a cobra must strike downward. Some snakes can open their mouths almost 180 degrees, with fangs sticking straight out, but not cobras. Their mouths open only 45 degrees. They must rise above their prey and strike downward to sink their short fangs through the skin.

From *Close Encounters with Deadly Dangers.* © 1998 Kendall Haven. Libraries Unlimited. (800) 237-6124.

The cobra dropped back to the grass with a sharp plop. Almost before I could blink its head rose again above the grass. It was closer this time. Close enough to strike, close enough for me to touch it if I stretched out my arm. I stared at the gently waving head, almost too frightened to breathe.

The cobra slowly spread its hood. I used to think it was just loose skin a cobra spread into the famous wide, flat hood at the back of its head, but my father told me it is actually a set of ribs the cobra can raise and flatten to push the skin out into a hood. My mother told me cobras do it to frighten their victims. Now I realized that it worked. I was *terrified*, especially when I remembered that cobras form a hood just before they strike.

My father's rifle was still in my hand. But I knew it was useless. Even if I had the gun raised and aimed, the cobra might well strike faster than I could squeeze the trigger.

Then the cobra began to hiss. Actually, it sounded very much like the sharp "shhhhh!" one person might hiss at another in a movie theater.

With deep dread I remembered that a hiss is the last thing a cobra does before it lunges at its victim.

I don't remember where the mongoose came from. It must have been sitting on the dirt bank above me. But faster than either the cobra or I could see, it raced past me and stopped next to the cobra.

A common mongoose, or meerkat, is about 16 inches long, with dense, coarse, brown-gray fur, small black toes and feet, and black hair around its eyes looking almost like a raccoon's mask. Many people keep a mongoose as a pet because these balls of fur love both to play and to be held.

A mongoose is also quick, far quicker than a cat. Some say a mongoose beats a cobra by tricking it. In a fight a mongoose bristles its thick fur and appears to be three times its actual size. The cobra strikes at the fur and misses the flesh, giving the mongoose a chance to grab the cobra's neck and head.

Some say the mongoose wins by outsmarting a cobra. With its head regally raised in the air, a cobra can't strike anything right next to its body, but must strike outward. There is a safe zone beside the cobra's coiled body. A mongoose somehow knows this, and is fast enough and small enough to reach this safe zone before it begins its own attack.

From *Close Encounters with Deadly Dangers*. © 1998 Kendall Haven. Libraries Unlimited. (800) 237-6124.

I don't know how; I just know that this mongoose saved my life when nothing else in the world could have. Before the cobra could change targets and lash forward with its deadly poison, the mongoose was at its throat, gripping the cobra's neck with all four feet. The mongoose savagely bit the cheek and lower jaw of the cobra. Then it darted back, stopping five or six feet from the cobra, panting to catch its breath. The whole attack lasted only three or four seconds.

As the cobra raised its wounded head, hissing in anger, the mongoose scampered in for a second time. Again it grabbed the cobra's neck and nipped and bit at its cheek, neck, and lower jaw. Again it sped back to safety to catch its breath.

Three times, four times, five, the mongoose fearlessly raced in a lightning-fast blur to attack this dreaded cobra over eight times its size. It moved and struck faster than I could see in the yellow moonlight.

It seemed to me that this deadly battle was a game to the mongoose, something it did for fun. Maybe the mongoose knew it *had* to kill cobras because the cobra would kill and eat it if it had the chance.

In less time than it would have taken for the cobra's venom to kill *me*, the cobra lay dead in the dry grass of the gully and my hero mongoose had scampered off.

Still shaking and dazed, I coiled the 40-pound cobra body over my shoulder and scrambled up the bank toward home.

Thinking About This Ecosystem

Are there predators who prey on big snakes like cobras? (*Young cobras have many enemies that prey on them. Full-grown cobras have only one predator: humans. But several animals, like the mongoose, will fight cobras, and will usually win.*)

Why do snakes need poison? When do they use it? (*Snakes use poison in two ways. First, they use it to more safely kill prey species. It only takes a second for a snake to dart in, inject poison, and race back out of reach of its victim. The snake is only vulnerable to counterattack by the claws, teeth, or beak of its victim for that one brief second. Then the snake can wait for its poison to kill or immobilize the prey before moving back in. Without poison, the snake would have to stay in contact with the prey much longer and would have to face far greater danger. Poison is a safer, easier way to subdue prey. A surprise attack with poison also lets snakes subdue speedy victims, such as rabbits, who are far too fast for the snake to ever catch and hold. Second, poison is used as a defensive weapon to both scare off and to kill potential predators or attacking animals or humans.*)

From *Close Encounters with Deadly Dangers*. © 1998 Kendall Haven. Libraries Unlimited. (800) 237-6124.

Are there other predators in the forests and jungles of India? Use the library and Internet to make a list of major predators in this ecosystem.

Thinking About This Predator

The four main species of cobras are spread across all of Africa, the Middle East, India, and large parts of China and the South Pacific. Cobras drink large quantities of water and so are never found in desert areas. Some of the small African cobras grow only to four feet. The scarce king cobras (found mostly in India and China) grow to 20 feet.

Cobras are unique for the "hood" they spread at the back of their heads when they rise up to strike. Why do you think they developed this capability? (*The hoods help to intimidate and terrify potential prey and, as a defense, to scare away potential predators. The hood makes the cobra appear bigger and more dangerous. It may also confuse a cobra's enemies. Bright circles on the back of the hood look like giant eyes and may discourage predators from attacking a cobra from behind by making them think that is really the cobra's front.*)

Some African cobras can spit their poison, accurately hitting a half-inch circle at a range of 10 feet. What advantages can you see to having this ability? (*It is safer for the cobra to deliver its poison without having to get near its prey and risk the injuries of a counterattack by claw or teeth.*)

Mongooses are a natural enemy of cobras. Cobras will eat a mongoose, but don't seek them out as a principal part of their diet. Mongooses don't eat cobras at all. Still, they seem naturally to know to fear and try to kill each other. Can you think of other natural enemies in different ecosystems? (*One other pair of natural enemies is mentioned in this book, the sperm whale and the giant squid. Look for others in your studies of different ecosystems and environments.*)

Here are some questions you can research about cobras in the library and on the Internet:

1. Why do snake charmers use cobras to dance high out of their baskets? What really mesmerizes the snake? How can the snake charmers better ensure their safety from deadly bites?

2. Most cobras are big snakes. What advantages and disadvantages do they gain from being big?

3. Cobras strike in a different way than most snakes do. Their fangs are shorter and their mouths don't open as wide. They don't coil and spring out, but rise up and strike downward. Make as complete a list as you can of the physical and behavioral differences between cobras and, for example, an American rattlesnake. Then search for advantages and disadvantages to each difference.

From Close Encounters with Deadly Dangers. © 1998 Kendall Haven. Libraries Unlimited. (800) 237-6124.

Additional Reading

Here are references for information about cobras and mongooses. See your librarian for additional titles available at your local library.

Bargar, Sherie. *Cobras*. Vero Beach, FL: Rourke Enterprises, 1986.

Ethan, Eric. *Cobras*. Milwaukee, WI: Gareth Stevens, 1995.

Fichter, George. *Poisonous Snakes*. New York: Franklin Watts, 1982.

Freeman, Russell. *Killer Snakes*. New York: Holiday House, 1982.

Hinton, H., and A. Dunn. *Mongooses: Their Natural History and Behavior*. Berkeley, CA: University of California Press, 1977.

Lloyd-Jones, W. "Habits of the Mongoose." *Journal of Bombay Natural History* 59 (1961): 695–728.

Mara, W. *Venomous Snakes of the World*. Neptune, NJ: T. H. F. Publications, 1993.

McCarthy, Colin. *Poisonous Snakes*. New York: Gloucester Press, 1987.

Minton, Sherman. *Venomous Reptiles*. New York: Charles Scribner's Sons, 1980.

Selsam, Millicent. *A First Look at Poisonous Snakes*. New York: Walker, 1987.

Simon, Seymour. *Poisonous Snakes*. New York: Four Winds Press, 1981.

Deadly Dragons

Komodo Dragons of Indonesia

At a Glance

Dragons! No word conjures such awe-inspiring and magical images as *dragons*! Dragons live at the heart of countless human myths, stories, and legends. Dragons are the most feared and yet fascinating of all mythical beasts.

It is surprising to find that, in our modern world of literal factuality, a real dragon exists on a half-dozen remote islands in the Indonesian chain, north of Australia. This real dragon has no wings, and is really one of the monitor lizards, the family of big lizards. By name, this monitor lizard is the Komodo dragon. Komodo is the name of the island on which they were first discovered by European explorers. The explorers called it a dragon because this great beast, 12 feet long and 350 pounds, was, in their minds, too big for the name "lizard."

Komodo dragons are fierce and cunning predators with all the guile, cunning, intelligence, and, yes, danger, anyone could want from a real dragon.

"Deadly Dragons"

The sun rose in a red ball over the South Pacific and swept its heat onto the Indonesian Island of Rintja, a tiny, eight-square-mile speck in an endless expanse of blue Pacific waves. To the northeast, Komodo Island and tiny Gili Morong Island rose like brown sharks' fins above the water. To the west, the larger Flores Island still hung in pre-dawn shadow.

The monsoons were over for the year. The long dry season was just settling in, gripping the land like a heavy, dusty fist for the next seven months. Streams would soon shrink. Watering holes would dry up. But the forests of Rintja were still lush and green.

Crows cawed greetings to the dawn. Toucans and monkeys chattered and howled. The thick forest felt cool and moist. It seemed to be a tropical island paradise, until the ground rumbled as the monster dragons awoke.

One by one, the great lizards crawled from their small holes. There were 600 on this island, only 5,000 in the whole world, all packed onto six small islands in Indonesia, north of Australia. These holes, far too small to be called caves, were either stolen from other animals and enlarged, or crudely dug with the dragons' great front claws, and barely protected the cold-blooded reptiles from the cool tropical nights.

A giant male Komodo dragon (named for the island on which they were first discovered), measuring 12 feet long and weighing over 300 pounds, lumbered stiffly into a clearing near his cave.

One species in the family of great monitor lizards, Komodo dragons are unlike every other lizard on earth. They are the biggest

From *Close Encounters with Deadly Dangers.* © 1998 Kendall Haven. Libraries Unlimited. (800) 237-6124.

living lizard. This Komodo dragon stood three feet tall with long, thick legs and neck. He had an alligator-like snout and rows of sharp, serrated teeth, like a shark. His skin looked like rusty chain mail with pebble-sized bumps, and hung in thick folds of dull red-brown around his throat, elbows, and knees. He was 15 years old, and would continue to grow as long as he lived, probably for another five years.

Komodo dragons don't display elaborate neck ruffles, spines, or horns. They don't need them. They are more like mean, street-fighting, neighborhood bullies than proud show-offs.

The dragon's body didn't touch the ground when he walked. Rather, he held it high, with only the tip of his tail and his four, wide feet leaving tracks in the trail behind him. Each foot sprouted five killer claws, each two inches around and five inches long. Excellent at digging, these claws could easily shred any animal on the island.

As the dragon reached his clearing, his need was not for food, but for heat. Komodo dragons, like all lizards, are cold blooded. He needed the sun's heat to keep his body temperature within functioning limits. He curled into a wide, bowl-shaped depression he had dug in the dirt to soak in the morning rays. In a typical day, a Komodo dragon spends 12 hours sleeping, seven hours heating or cooling to control his body temperature (thermal regulating), five hours hunting, and seven minutes eating.

By mid-morning his body had warmed to optimal temperature. Now he remembered how hungry he was. He had not eaten yesterday, and had not had a large meal, like a whole deer, for almost a week.

He lumbered from the clearing and started down the trails that led to the forested and grass-covered valleys below. Like all Komodo dragons, he did most of his hunting mid-morning and mid-afternoon. He had to. Mid-day was too hot to hunt, so he spent that time making sure he didn't overheat. Nights and mornings were too cold, so he either slept to conserve heat or sunned to soak in the heat he desperately needed.

When he was young, the dragon had climbed trees, jumping from limb to limb to chase down monkeys and squirrels. He could still climb, using his sharp claws to dig into tree trunks, but he rarely did. He was too big now to catch anything in the trees.

Stomping down the trail, body and tail bending, curving with every step like an alligator's, he planned his hunting strategy.

From *Close Encounters with Deadly Dangers.* © 1998 Kendall Haven. Libraries Unlimited. (800) 237-6124.

Komodo dragons are the most intelligent living lizard and very capable of planning a successful ambush.

The lizard passed tall stands of bamboo and towering tamarind trees to reach a lush field of waving themeder grass. Almost six feet tall and just starting to yellow with the onset of the dry season, the grass would be a powerful attraction to grazing deer and a perfect hiding place for the lizard. Komodo dragons can run at 10 to 15 miles per hour, but only for short bursts. They would rather surprise their prey in a sudden, violent rush of only a few feet.

The lizard paused in the tree line and raised his head, pushing up with his front legs. He scanned the wide grass field, his head now five and one-half feet in the air. A Komodo dragon's neck is extremely flexible, so that he can turn his head to see everywhere without moving his great body.

He spotted a meandering trail through the grass and decided to set his trap there. Carefully edging through the field, staying downwind of any unsuspecting prey, he edged to within a foot of the trail. He trampled enough grass to allow him to lie flat, head stretched out and pointing at the path, hidden by a narrow line of tall grass.

Now he would wait. His only worry was that he might overheat in this bright sunlight before he had a chance to make a killing strike.

If he were lucky a deer, wild boar, or water buffalo would wander by, but a smaller Komodo dragon would do just as well. Few Komodo dragons ever reach old age. Most are eaten by other dragons.

Most who aren't eaten eventually starve. As the dry season progressed, food always became scarce. During the dry season a snake, rat, chicken, or even a crab on the beach would be a real prize.

Komodo dragons hunt by smell. Their eyesight is good, but they are practically deaf. They can smell a dead animal eight miles away.

Dragons don't smell with their noses. They are equipped with chemical sensing organs called Jacobson's organs, nestled into the roof of their mouths.

The lizards' three-foot-long, yellow tongues constantly slither in and out to taste the air. Actually, the tips of their forked tongues collect molecules of air and pull them back into the Jacobson's organs.

The dragon's tongue slowly flicked in and out as he lay in hiding. After an hour he picked up the scent of deer. In 15 minutes he could feel the vibrations of their hooves as they strolled down his path. He had chosen his ambush spot wisely today.

From *Close Encounters with Deadly Dangers*. © 1998 Kendall Haven. Libraries Unlimited. (800) 237-6124.

Still he waited.

The deer, two does with a strapping buck in the lead, nibbled their way along the path and toward a watering hole across the valley. All seemed quiet. All seemed safe.

Then the grass exploded next to the buck. The deer reared and sprang for safety as 10 gleaming claws and a great spread of teeth, with saliva dripping from each jagged tooth, sprang at his flank.

The buck was rocked by the impact and stumbled as he sped for safety. The dragon's great teeth, while opening a long wound on the deer's shoulder, did not find a solid hold. One set of claws raked the buck's flank. The other barely touched its cheek.

The other two deer bolted in terror as the Komodo dragon crashed to the trail. His meal had escaped, but the dragon didn't mind. His attack had done its job. The buck might bleed to death this afternoon and be a delicious dinner tonight or tomorrow. If it didn't bleed to death, the festering wounds would surely kill it within a few days.

The ultimate weapon of the Komodo dragon is its saliva. Filled with strong bacteria, this saliva prevents a wound from closing and healing. A Komodo dragon's tendency to drool heavily while on the hunt means that any small scrape or wound it inflicts will be life threatening.

As the dragon rumbled toward the watering hole, its vibrations disturbed a large viper snake slithering across the path toward its hole.

One dragon foot slammed down on the snake's tail. It coiled, hissed, and turned to attack. But viper fangs can't penetrate a dragon's thick skin. A second dragon foot crashed down on the snake's head. He grabbed the snake in his teeth and, with a strong jerk, ripped it in half. He quickly gobbled both halves of the poisonous snake and continued toward cool shade and water.

By now the dragon was overheating. He needed to cool quickly. If his body temperature rose above 108 degrees Fahrenheit, he could die. He opened his giant mouth and began to pant as he reached the shade of tamarind trees. He plunged into muddy water, scooping a great mouthful. Raising his head, he let the cool water run down his throat to cool his body.

By mid-afternoon he was ready to hunt again. He rose as high as he could, tongue flicking through the air to taste it. He sensed dead

From *Close Encounters with Deadly Dangers.* © 1998 Kendall Haven. Libraries Unlimited. (800) 237-6124.

meat, a large water buffalo, dead less than a day and not more than two miles away.

Komodo dragons prefer dead meat. They would rather scavenge than hunt. To a dragon, the putrid oils radiating from decaying flesh are the sweet aroma of a favorite treat. The only danger of such a carrion feast would be other Komodo dragons that might show up. Larger dragons are as likely to eat a smaller dragon as the dead animal that drew them to the spot.

A female dragon, about 10 feet long, arrived at the dead buffalo just before the male. A festering gash on the buffalo's flank from an old dragon attack was the obvious cause of death.

The female focused on tearing open the buffalo's stomach, a dragon's favorite part. With legs braced, she ripped a large chunk of flesh loose, burying her head and shoulders in the fallen animal's innards.

The male rushed in and seized a mouthful of buffalo flank. The startled female jumped back. Both large dragons hissed at each other, stretching their mouths wide. All adult dragons carry long slashing scars from previous fights and brawls. Many of the fights end in death for one or both dragons. Both dragons arched their bodies sideways and curled their thick tails, ready to strike.

A smaller, five-year-old Komodo dragon saw her chance and darted in from the bushes to attack the buffalo's chest and shoulder. Both large dragons abandoned their standoff to make sure they didn't miss the feast. Every dragon now tried simply to swallow as much food as possible before the next dragon got it. With violent tearing motions, they ripped flesh and bone from the carcass and swallowed without chewing. Thirty or forty pounds of buffalo disappeared in a single swallow.

The young dragon scampered off before either larger dragon could decide to feast on her. The two larger dragons stayed to finish the job, devouring every morsel. Their heads and forelegs were covered with blood and gristle.

With a final hiss of warning, the male sauntered uphill toward his hole. He was now too full to care about fighting, and didn't dare risk overheating during an afternoon battle. He walked slowly, beginning to digest his meal, making sure he didn't overheat during his climb.

The sun set in a fiery red ball over the South Pacific as he reached his crude hole. Crows cawed farewell to the day. Toucans and monkeys chattered and howled at the rising moon. The thick monsoon forest felt cool and moist. Another day had ended in paradise, and soon the dragons were all asleep.

Thinking About This Ecosystem

The Komodo dragon lives on islands described as a "monsoon forest ecosystem." Is a monsoon forest different from a rain forest? If so, how? (*Rain forests get rain through most of the year. Their dry seasons are short and do not completely dry out the forest. Monsoon forests may receive almost as much rain over the course of a year, but the rain comes much more seasonally. During the short monsoon period rain falls in torrents. This is followed by a long dry season during which plants do dry out and are water-stressed.*)

What role do the dragons play in this ecosystem? (*Komodo dragons are the top predator for this ecosystem.*) What do you think would happen if all the dragons were removed or killed? (*The species dragons feed on—deer, wild boars, rats, snakes, goats, and buffalo—would tend to overpopulate because there would no longer be any control on their population. This grazer overpopulation would over-stress grass supplies and kill much of the natural grass. There would follow a large-scale die-off as grazer species starved to death. Limited food supply, instead of predators, would finally control a new level of stable grazer population.*)

Use the library and the Internet to find out how grazers in a small island environment survive the long dry season. Where can they find food and water?

Thinking About This Predator

Komodo dragons act like brutal bullies. They eat like slobs, have no family ties or loyalties, and stomp through the forests as if looking for a fight. They attack anything and everything, including other dragons. Most dragons are killed by other dragons. Few reach old age.

Young Komodo dragons are excellent tree climbers. They use this skill both to hunt prey species that the bigger adult dragons ignore and to escape from hungry adult dragons. As young dragons grow and lose the yellow and green stripes and speckled spots of youth, it must be frightening to come down out of the trees and face the other dragons who have been, and still are, the greatest danger young dragons will ever face.

Why do you think such a giant lizard ever evolved on such small islands with a limited food supply? (*The most popular theory is that ancient island lizards grew larger and larger to be able to prey on a species of pygmy elephant that*

From *Close Encounters with Deadly Dangers.* © 1998 Kendall Haven. Libraries Unlimited. (800) 237-6124.

flourished on the islands. The elephants became extinct centuries ago. Most now believe that Komodo dragons killed and ate all the pygmy elephants.)

Here are some questions you can research about Komodo dragons in the library and on the Internet:

1. Do you think Komodo dragons should be called "dragons?" In what ways are they similar to your image of a dragon? In what ways are they dissimilar?

2. Why do you think Komodo dragons so readily attack and eat younger, smaller Komodo dragons? Do you think this is good or bad for the survival of the species?

Additional Reading

Here are references for information about Komodo dragons and the monsoon jungle ecosystem. See your librarian for additional titles available at your local library.

Auffenberg, Walter. *The Behavioral Ecology of the Komodo Monitor.* Gainesville, FL: University Presses of Florida, 1981.

Bellairs, Angus. *The Life of Reptiles, Vol. 2.* New York: Universe Books, 1970.

Darling, Kathy. *Komodo Dragon.* New York: Lothrop, Lee & Shepard, 1993.

DePrato, Mario. *Twentieth Century Dragons: Varanus Komodoensis.* Washington, DC: National Zoological Park, 1985.

Diamond, Jarad. "Natural Selection: Did Komodo Dragons Evolve to Eat Pigmy Elephants?" *Nature* 326 (1987): 832–36.

Hopf, Alice. *Biology of the Komodo Dragon.* New York: Putnam, 1981.

Kern, James. "Dragon Lizards of Komodo." *National Geographic* 154 (6) (December, 1968): 872–80.

King, F. "The Giant Lizards of Komodo." *Nature and Science* 38 (September 15, 1969): 5–7.

Lutz, Dick, and Marie Lutz. *Komodo: The Living Dragon.* Salem, OR: Dimi Press, 1991.

Martin, James. *Komodo Dragons: Giant Lizards of Indonesia.* Minneapolis, MN: Capstone Press, 1995.

Mertens, Robert. *The World of Amphibians and Reptiles.* London: George Harrap, 1960.

Minton, Sherman. *Giant Reptiles.* New York: Charles Scribner's Sons, 1973.

Osman, Hilmi. "A Note on the Breeding Behavior of the Komodo Dragons." *International Zoo Yearbook* 7 (1967): 10–11.

Watson, Lyall. *The Dreams of Dragons.* New York: William Morrow, 1987.

Lions & Tigers & Bears

Siberian Tigers of Northern China

At a Glance

The word *tiger* brings up images of striped, snarling man-eaters roaming invisibly through lush jungles. Tigers are the greatest of all the great cats: fast, agile, quick, and deadly.

Siberian tigers, the biggest and greatest of all the tigers, live in a very different climate. Winters for the Siberian tiger reach minus 50 degrees Fahrenheit. There is no red or orange in the thick winter coat of a Siberian. In winter they are white with black stripes and dots, to match their snowy surroundings.

Siberians are always on the move through their vast territories in search of food. Tagged Siberians have traveled 620 miles in 22 days to find enough to eat. These tigers need to eat over 30 pounds of food per day just to sustain life in their harsh winter environment.

Siberian tigers live on the edge, just barely able to sustain a living in a harsh environment other predators couldn't tolerate. This is an environment where the right to live is measured by the ability to catch food, day in and day out, and where any injury, even a seemingly minor one like a thorn in a paw or a cold, can be life threatening, because the wound makes it harder to hunt. Often that little edge is all that separates a Siberian tiger from starvation.

It is a harsh, cold world the Siberian tiger lives in, but also a world of breathtaking beauty. Siberian tigers are a harsh top predator in that world, but also animals of boundless grace and beauty.

"Lions & Tigers & Bears"

He was a tiger. He had never known fear or doubt. Actually, he was still a cub, barely five months old, and the reckless boldness with which he lived his young life was a constant worry to his mother.

She knew the dangers. Young tigers *do* have enemies, and they risk crippling accidents as their play grows rougher. She had two cubs, one female and one male. It was this young male with three black dots between the stripes across his cheek who refused to recognize the cautions, the warning signs, and the dangers, even when she swatted him with her massive paw to help him remember.

If he survived to be an adult Siberian tiger, the largest and greatest cat in the world, he would have only one enemy: other male Siberians. But he still had over a year of growing and training before he could survive on his own, and there were times when she didn't think he would survive the day.

A male Siberian tiger can grow to 12 feet from nose to tail and can weigh 650 pounds: Over a quarter ton of muscled power, grace, beauty, and agility. The cub with three dots was still 90 pounds of awkward clumsiness.

Over twice the size of the better known Bengal tiger, Siberians have white bellies with pale yellow to tan fur marked with black stripes, dots, and dashes, and yellow, luminous eyes. Like fingerprints for a human, each tiger has a unique pattern of stripes and dots. Over half of all tiger species are now extinct. Siberians have survived only because of the remoteness of their shrinking territory: the mountains of southwest Siberia, North Korea, and northeast China.

From *Close Encounters with Deadly Dangers.* © 1998 Kendall Haven. Libraries Unlimited. (800) 237-6124.

As his mother napped in the warm morning sun, the three-dot cub scampered through the underbrush of the sloping pine forest around their den. He heard heavy breathing, twigs snapping, and bushes being roughly shoved aside. He saw shadowed movement through the trees and undergrowth.

Three-Dot dropped to a crouch and began to slither forward, staring at the growling hulk through the bushes, stalking as if this unknown intruder were his favorite meal.

Three-Dot's small claws naturally extended, as do those of all tigers when they are on the hunt. His eyes gleamed with the excitement of pursuit as his legs steadily crept forward, little muscles tensed.

A 300-pound black bear, still snarling over some past failure, shouldered through the bushes and stopped face-to-face with the hissing, 90-pound striped fur ball.

Three-Dot's ears were pinned back in anger. He hissed and spit his warning at the invader.

The bear roared a blast that shook the trees, rising up on his hind legs to crash down and crush the upstart, its long claws pawing the air. To fearless Three-Dot, this looked like a perfect opportunity to attack the bear's hind leg.

Behind him, Three-Dot heard a sharp grunt. He knew it was his mother's call. He recognized her voice and her smell. Besides, she was the only adult tiger he had ever seen. Her grunt was a demand for instant obedience. Still Three-Dot hesitated, unwilling to give up this prize he had so cleverly stalked and cornered.

Again he heard the grunt, more insistent this time. Tigers are not loud animals. They do not like to roar as do lions and bears. A sharp grunt from his mother was the same as a thunderous, ear-splitting shriek from some other species.

With a final, disappointed hiss, Three-Dot turned and trotted back to the den. The bear dropped to all fours and continued its angry march toward the river.

Three-Dot's mother growled as he scampered to her. Her nose and forehead wrinkled in anger. She hissed and swatted him so hard he tumbled head-over-heels into a pine trunk. Would he never learn which animals could cause him harm?

Three-Dot sat alone by the den and moaned, as tigers will after failure. He thought not of his mother's scolding, but of his lost prize

From *Close Encounters with Deadly Dangers.* © 1998 Kendall Haven. Libraries Unlimited. (800) 237-6124.

and of how proud he would have been standing over the great kill when his mother and sister found him.

Siberian tigers live solitary lives and must learn to be totally self-sufficient. There isn't enough food in their harsh, mountain territory to support *families* of tigers. A single male tiger will stake out an area of hundreds of square miles as his solitary kingdom. Females are allowed to adopt small plots at the edge of a male's domain. They also live alone, or with their cubs for the first 12 to 18 months of the cubs' lives. A male tolerates his chosen females, but would attack all others, including his own offspring, if he met them on a forest path. A tigress must protect, feed, and teach her young all by herself if they are to survive.

By the time it is six months old and weighs 100 pounds, a cub should have become a serious hunter. Three-Dot's sister was already able to catch small game and fish. Three-Dot would rather play than patiently stalk a deer. He would still rather attack a bear who could kill him than a hare he could eat.

Tigers do most of their hunting at night. Sounds carry farther then. Tigers' excellent night vision gives them their biggest advantage over prey. A tiger's night vision is over five times as good as the best human's.

However, a tiger will hunt anytime if hunger and opportunity call for it. The mother tiger stretched and rose in mid-afternoon. The family would hunt now. Three-Dot needed all the practice he could get.

Her two cubs followed single file along well-worn trails. Many of these trails had been made by the resident male tiger, who had also marked them with his scent, regular, deep claw marks on the trees, and parallel lines drawn in the dirt with his paw.

These markings were there to warn other male Siberian tigers away. If two males met, a battle would surely follow. One or both would be seriously injured. An injured tiger can't hunt, and a tiger needs 30 or more pounds of food a day to survive, especially during the bitter cold winter. Injured tigers often starve before they heal. So a male marks his territory very well.

The mother stopped, tail twitching, ears pricked tall, straining to locate a sound. Three-Dot's sister mirrored her mother. Three-Dot sat and scratched behind his ear, waiting for his mother to locate their prey.

From *Close Encounters with Deadly Dangers.* © 1998 Kendall Haven. Libraries Unlimited. (800) 237-6124.

She grunted low.

Three-Dot dutifully rose and cocked his head to locate and identify the sound. Tigers rely on their exceptional vision when they can, but tall grass and thick undergrowth makes seeing difficult.

His sister seemed to have figured out the sound and slinked forward in a stalking crouch, pushing through the grass almost on her belly. Three-Dot followed in her footsteps.

Tigers prefer hunting in thick grass because it so perfectly matches their stripes. Slinking through grass, a tiger is invisible. The only sign that it has passed is the soft rippling of the grass as if a sudden breeze had blown.

The cubs' mother slunk beside them, guiding their attack. Two chital deer grazed quietly across the meadow. Both were probably too big for her cubs to bring down, but it would be valuable training for them to try.

Sister in the lead, both cubs slithered forward, curved claws extended. Their goal was to get within 30 feet, then dash forward and slam into the prey to knock it off its feet before it could bolt and run. Finally, they would pounce and grab the animal with their mighty teeth, preferably in the neck. A tiger's four long fangs do the real work of an attack. They are massive upper fangs, with long lower canines, and they slam shut in a killing grip.

Closer crept the three hunters as the grass whispered and waved.

Three-Dot began to wonder how close they were and if it was time to pounce yet. What was it they were stalking, anyway? What did it look like? Had it heard them coming? He paused and raised his head above the grass for a good peek.

The mother grunted low and sharply cuffed him. He "woof-ed" in surprise and dropped back down to a stalking crouch. She wrinkled her nose and glared at him as if to yell, "Pay attention to what you're doing!"

Three-Dot heard a rustling noise through the grass. His head turned, then snapped back. *Pay attention to the hunt.*

But there it was again, soft rustling moving away from him through the grass. Maybe that was what they were supposed to be hunting. Maybe it was escaping.

He veered left to investigate. The waving grasses parted around Three-Dot's nose and powerful shoulders as he passed. He crept

From *Close Encounters with Deadly Dangers.* © 1998 Kendall Haven. Libraries Unlimited. (800) 237-6124.

steadily toward the rustling sound, soft and low, obviously made by a small animal just ahead. Three-Dot would show his mother and sister what a good hunter he was. He would catch whatever this was, and still make it back in time to help stalk the deer.

Closer and closer. He could almost see it through the grass ahead. Three-Dot dropped to his belly and crawled forward, inches at a time. He saw a tail with bristly spines. He saw a small, round body. He pounced forward and landed with one paw on top of a porcupine.

"Woof!" he yelped in surprise as searing pain shot through his paw. Three-Dot bounded into the air, shaking his paw.

Both deer froze, staring at the bouncing tiger. Then both bolted for the safety of the forest.

The sister cub hissed at her lost meal and sprang after the deer for a few steps, knowing even as she did so that deer can easily outrun even a full-grown tiger.

The mother purred and nuzzled her daughter. She, at least, would be an excellent hunter. The female cub meowed in appreciation of the praise.

Then the mother grunted and swatted Three-Dot to help him learn both to concentrate on his hunting and to stay away from porcupines. She helped him remove the three quills from his paw and lick the wound. If one got infected, Three-Dot wouldn't be able to run, maybe not even to walk. If he couldn't run, he couldn't hunt. Without hunting, he couldn't eat or survive. No, a tiger *never* wanted to fool around with a porcupine.

She swatted him again to help him remember.

On the path ahead they heard a deep, rumbling growl. A male Siberian tiger was approaching. The mother harshly nudged her children and grunted to herd them away from this terrible danger.

Three-Dot bristled and spread his front legs in the path, challenging this still-unseen intruder. He hissed out a warning.

The mother grunted and gave him a sharp swat as he stood his ground, hissing in the path. "Follow me *now!*" the swat commanded.

Three-Dot wrinkled his nose and hissed a final warning at the stranger. From beyond a bend in the trail he heard a deep, rumbling hiss in answer to his challenge.

Mother softly swatted him again as a final reminder as he reluctantly followed her into the safety of the forest. "Oh, you don't want to meet a full-grown male Siberian tiger," the swat said. "You would surely die."

Won't he ever learn?

As the sun dipped low toward the western peaks, the mother herded her children toward the river for a drink before they took up again the endless search for food and survival.

Thinking About This Ecosystem

Ecosystem food webs are often described as being shaped like a pyramid. A great mass of grass and plants occupies the thick bottom of this pyramid. A thinner mass of grazers is above this layer. A much smaller mass of predators is above this, and a tiny triangular space is left at the top for the top predators. This means that a great mass of plants and grazers is required to support a very few top predators. How is this relationship evident in the lifestyle of Siberian tigers? (*Each male tiger stakes claim to a territory of many hundreds, or even thousands of acres and will not permit another male to enter this domain. That is a lot of space to support just one tiger. Even with all this vast space, many tigers barely survive.*)

Why do you think the Siberian tiger is so territorial? (*Each tiger needs 30 or more pounds of food each day. It takes a very large land area in this ecosystem to produce enough grazers to support the tiger's food needs. Tigers are fiercely territorial because they cannot afford to share their already marginal food supplies.*) Can you think of other territorial predators? Can you think of some that are not very territorial? (*Most predators, even insect predators, are territorial to some degree. Fish and whales are as close to non-territorial predators as can be found. The real question is the* degree *to which a predator tolerates others to pass through or temporarily use the region that the predator claims as its own.*) Use the resources of the library and the Internet to help in your search.

Why do you think a male Siberian allows several females to use corners of his territory? (*The male needs available females to procreate and pass on his genes, his life force. It is easier and more successful to allow females to live in his land than it is to search for them when the tiger is ready to mate.*) Do other male predators act this way? Can you find other examples?

Thinking About This Predator

Each individual tiger, including the Siberian tiger, has a unique pattern of black stripes and facial dots, just as each human has a unique pattern of fingerprints. It is believed that tigers recognize and identify other tigers by their stripe patterns.

From *Close Encounters with Deadly Dangers*. © 1998 Kendall Haven. Libraries Unlimited. (800) 237-6124.

Male Siberian tigers are the most solitary of all predators. After leaving their mothers at the age of two, they live the rest of their 25-year lives alone. Each male claims and marks huge territories to have enough food to eat without collapsing the prey populations that support him. Siberians have been measured traveling 40 and even 50 miles each day in search of food. Siberians are incredibly strong and can drag a dead carcass that would take more than a dozen people to move. Siberians, the biggest cats on earth, can also eat over 100 pounds of meat in a single meal.

There used to be eight tiger species on Earth. Three have been hunted to extinction. All of the remaining five are designated as endangered (in danger of becoming extinct). Because of their great size (hunters try for the biggest and fiercest), all Siberian tigers would surely have been hunted down were it not for the remoteness and harshness of their habitat.

Here are some questions you can research about Siberian tigers in the library and on the Internet:

1. Why do you think male Siberian tigers permit one or two females to live in their territory, but will attack their own offspring if they should meet?

2. Why do you think Siberian tigers are willing to live in such a harsh environment instead of forcing their way into the warmer lowlands where more game would be available for them to eat?

Additional Reading

Here are references for information about Siberian tigers and their forest ecosystem. See your librarian for additional titles available at your local library.

Arjan, Singh. *Tiger! Tiger!* London: J. Cape, 1984.

Barnes, Simon. *Tiger!* New York: St. Martin's Press, 1994.

Bender, Lionel. *Lions and Tigers.* New York: Gloucester Press, 1988.

Biel, Timothy. *Tigers.* Mankato, MN: Creative Education, 1990.

Bright, Michael. *Tiger.* New York: Gloucester Press, 1989.

Cajacob, Thomas. *Close to the Wild: Siberian Tigers in a Zoo.* Minneapolis, MN: Carolrhoda Books, 1986.

DuTemple, Lesley. *Tigers.* Minneapolis, MN: Lerner Publications, 1996.

Hewett, Joan. *Tiger, Tiger, Growing Up.* New York: Clarion Books, 1993.

Hoffman, Mary. *Tiger.* Milwaukee, WI: Raintree Children's Books, 1984.

Hunt, Patricia. *Tigers.* New York: Dodd, Mead, 1981.

Jacobson, Peter. *Tigers*. Secaucus, NJ: Chartwell Books, 1990.

Lavine, Sigmund. *Wonders of Tigers*. New York: Dodd, Mead, 1987.

Lerner, Ted. *Tiger Trek*. New York: Macmillan, 1990.

Plunkrose, Henry. *Lions and Tigers*. New York: Gloucester Press, 1979.

Royston, Angela. *The Tiger*. New York: Warwick Press, 1988.

Schaller, George, and Millicent Selsam. *The Tiger: Its Life in the Wild*. New York: Harper & Row, 1979.

Stone, Lynn. *The Tiger*. Vero Beach, FL: Rourke Enterprises, 1989.

Thapar, Valmik. *The Tiger's Destiny*. London: Kyle Cathie Books, 1992.

Urquhart, Jennifer. *The Big Cats*. Washington, DC: National Geographic Society, 1990.

Index

About the Author

A former research scientist, Kendall Haven is the only West Point graduate to ever become a professional storyteller. He holds a Master's Degree in Oceanography and spent six years with the Department of Energy before finding his true passion for storytelling and a very different kind of "truth." He has now performed for close to 3 million people in 40 states, and has won awards for his story-writing and storytelling. He has conducted workshops in over 20 states on storytelling's practical, in-class teaching power, and has become one of the nation's leading advocates for the educational value of storytelling.

Kendall has recorded five audio tapes and published six books of original stories. He has also used his writing talent to create stories for many non-profit organizations, including The American Cancer Society and the Institute for Mental Health Initiatives. He recently created a national award-winning adventure drama for National Public Radio on the effects of watching television. His first Teacher Ideas Press book of 50 science stories, *Marvels of Science*, makes the history and process of science fascinating and compelling. *Amazing American Women* illuminates 40 fascinating and little known women's stories in American history. His third book, *Great Moments in Science*, was released in early 1996. Haven continues to develop other books.

Haven's most recent awards include the 1995 and 1996 Storytelling World Silver Award for best Story Anthology, the 1993 International Festival Association Silver Award for best Education Program, the 1992 Corporation for Public Broadcasting Silver Award for best Children's Public Radio Production, and the 1991 Award for Excellence in California Education. He has twice been an American Library Association "Notable Recording Artist," and is the only storyteller in the United States with three entries in the ALA's *Best of the Best for Children*.

Haven is founder and Chair of the International Whole Language Umbrella Storytelling Interest Group, and is on the Board of Directors as well as the Educational Advisory Committee of the National Storytelling Association. He is a co-director of the Sonoma Storytelling Festival, past four-year Chair of the Bay Area Storytelling Festival, and founder of storytelling festivals in Las Vegas, NV; Boise, ID; and Mariposa, CA.

He lives with his wife in the rolling Sonoma County grape vineyards in rural Northern California.

149